D1710716

MERCEDES-BENZ 300
1951-62

Schiffer Automotive Series

MERCEDES-BENZ 300

Sedans, Coupes, Cabriolets

1951-62

A Documentation by Walter Zeichner

Schiffer Publishing Ltd

1469 Morstein Road, West Chester, Pennsylvania 19380

This volume of the Schiffer Automotive Series is dedicated to the famous Mercedes 300, the prestige car from the house of Daimler-Benz later known as the "Adenauer-Car." The three-liter car, praised in the Fifties as a car of superlatives, was not only a model of German automobile production but also a status symbol and the embodiment of the highest esteem. One had respect for the car, and usually for its passengers too. When you look through this volume, a lot of nostalgia will come alive, which was its purpose, rather than offering owners of a 300 help with restoration.

Thanks for their support in assembling the materials are extended to Kai Jacobsen, Georg Amtmann, H. P. Rinsma and Robert Horender, who also compiled the list of miniature models of the Type 300.

Halwart Schrader
Editor

Translated from the German by Dr. Edward Force,
Central Connecticut State University.

Printed in the United States of America.
ISBN: 0-88740-249-6

This book originally published under the title,
Mercedes-Benz 300 1951-62,
by Schrader Automobil Bücher,
Handels-GmbH, München.
© 1987. ISBN: 3-922617-21-2.

Published by Schiffer Publishing, Ltd.
1469 Morstein Road
West Chester, Pennsylvania 19380
Please write for a free catalog.
This book may be purchased from the publisher.
Please include $2.00 postage.
Try your bookstore first.

Contents

Mercedes 300—The Prestige Car

Before the 1951 Frankfurt Auto Show opened its doors, the German automobile industry could show a remarkably positive balance for the previous year. Almost all the automobile factories that had been partially destroyed in the war had taken up car production again. With a total of 219,409 units, the previous year's production had been more than doubled, and the whole economy was growing quickly. Naturally, the most successful manufacturer was the firm of Volkswagen, the very symbol of the rebuilding of German industry, and many competitors also tried to produce vehicles for the broad masses. But the trick was to build them even better and less expensively. The time of many small cars began.

It was also a time of contrasts, as the Mercedes-Benz 300, almost five meters long, was introduced to a public that, in most cases, still had to dream of being able to buy a car and was happy if their income sufficed to get a sidecar for their used motorcycle. At the same time as one could push a button on the dashboard of the Mercedes 300 to activate auxiliary springs that evened out heavy loads in the car, the constructors of the 10-HP Lloyd 300, at their factory in Bremen, were wondering how they could replace at least part of the wooden body of their little car, covered in imitation leather, with sheet metal parts.

This new Mercedes belonged in another world, being much more unattainable than luxury cars are for the present-day average customer. As early as 1946, production of the prewar Type 170, only slightly changed, had begun at the Stuttgart factory, in order to profit from the marque's excellent reputation before the war. As did Opel and Ford in these first postwar years, Daimler-Benz also wasted no energy developing a new body, but concentrated on making the technology and equipment of the car

suit the growing demands of the customers. The great venture came only in 1951 with the simultaneous introduction of the 220 and 300 models in Frankfurt. The six-cylinder 220 model still closely resembled the Type 170 and, despite a heavier and considerably lengthened body, still conformed to the typical appearance of a prewar car. Early studies for the planned Type 300 also show a close adherence on the part of the designers to the aesthetic ideals of times past; in comparison to the 220, though, these efforts resulted only in a lengthened wheelbase and a small, straight windshield. Even free-standing headlights would have amounted to a step backward into the styles of the Thirties.

Fortunately, though, it was finally decided to give the "flagship" of the world's oldest automobile manufacturer, which went into series production in November of 1951, a body that, despite many suggestions of the glorious days of old, showed clean modern lines and large window areas.

As seen at the Frankfurt Salon, the mighty sedan naturally inspired description as a "heavy car." Of course the continuing window lines on the sides and the fender curves that flowed almost to the ends of the front doors—especially as seen from the side—took away much of the air of weightiness and even afforded a hint of sportiness, but if one approached the 300 from the front or the rear, its width and height made clear that the car was a "monument on wheels."

At the front end, the upright, almost Gothic radiator grille formed a barrier between the inhabitants and the rest of the world, and a slim rear window provided protection against curious followers. After opening the heavy, richly chromed driver's door, one did not sit down into the car; one climbed into it almost as into a coach, a type of

One of the greatest prestige cars made by Mercedes-Benz in the Thirties was the Type 500 Nürburg. Its displacement was lavish—the straight-eight motor had a volume of five liters. At right is a 3.2 liter of 1937.

acquaintance that may seem completely foreign to the consumers of modern mass-produced goods. Though a tall person is lucky today to get into a car without hitting his head, in those days it was perfectly normal to enter the interior of a Mercedes-Benz 300 with a hat on, an important point for official and formal occasions, for which these sedans were frequently used. When one seats himself on the high, comfortable, well-formed driver's seat, covered with costly materials, one has a gigantic steering wheel, 44cm in diameter and otherwise found only in trucks, before one, with the famous star in the middle, surrounded by a chromed horn ring which also serves as the flasher control. The two-tone dashboard under the slightly arched windshield dates from before the times when manufacturers gave much thought to the safety of the passengers in an accident. and affords plenty of play with a large assortment of gleaming chrome knobs, switches and levers. In addition to the usual controls for windshield wipers, starter and lights, one could also use these controls to provide additional springing for the rear axle, choose between two- and three-tone horn fanfares, activate the central lubrication to supply important parts with grease, and adjust the

motor to the octane rating of the gasoline, which was still of very varying quality during the Fifties. On the other hand, the instruments to indicate speed, oil pressure, water temperature, fuel level and battery charging were simple and factual. The tachometer, round and clear, was right in front of the driver, with the other instruments gathered in horizontal groups to the left and right of it. All the control switches gave the impression of being, and proved in practice to be, of unusually good quality and large size, so that the people traveling in this car could always have a feeling of security and confidence in its highly developed, reliable technology.

The Type 300 was not produced in great numbers; this could be seen in the absolutely precise workmanship in the interior. There were no sloppily made details in dark corners; everything seemed to have been built for eternity. But this car held an

7

The 1937-38 Mercedes-Benz 320 as a two-seat sports Cabriolet A. This car can be compared to the later 300 Sc of the Fifties—a few styling elements can easily be recognized in the postwar car.

uncontested top position not only because of its comfortable furnishings, unequaled even in Germany. Daimler-Benz had created a masterpiece in terms of the chassis too. Based on the old established X-shaped oval tube frame that provided a maximum of stability at a low weight, the front wheels were independently suspended by double transverse links, coil springs and anti-roll bar, while the rear axle took the form of a swing axle with double coil springs and could be adapted for heavy loads by activating an electrically activated torsion-bar suspension in order to regulate the car's balance.

Along with a wheelbase of fully three meters, these features provided a suspension and driving comfort such as was practically unknown until then, and also awakened the rear swing axle, especially in fast driving on winding roads, giving the passengers in the back seats an occasional floating feeling in the stomach.

This mass of car, weighing almost 1.8 tons dry, was powered by a straight six-cylinder motor that stood out in both sturdiness and sportiness. With a low compression of only 6.4:1, this short-stroke powerplant produced 115 HP at 4600 rpm of the seven-bearing crankshaft, which was no great problem for the high weight of the car. By the standards of the time, the 1951 300 produced quite extraordinary performance. It reached the 100-kph mark in 18 seconds, and a top speed of about 160 kph meant that even the most powerful Porsche of the time would have to be pushed to its limits to keep up with the heavy sedan. So as not to expose the motor to greater wear in cold weather, there was a heat exchanger in the cooling water that warmed the motor oil quickly after the motor was started.

All of these features not only made the Mercedes 300 a first-rank prestige car, but also guaranteed the more down-to-earth driver a high degree of pleasant and safe driving in everyday traffic with this car.

Remarkably, Daimler-Benz had by no means exhausted the luxury market when it put the Type 300 into production. Whoever was ready to pay 3800

Marks more than the basic price could order his 300 as a four-door Cabriolet D and thus own one of the most desirable cars of early postwar days. Only a few specimens, carefully handmade, left the factory per month and offered up to five people the pleasure of top-down driving. This precisely functioning, gigantic top was a masterpiece of precision and expert handiwork, and when raised, it enveloped the

In 1950 styling experiments were undertaken to find the right lines for the 300. Note the similarities in form between these prototypes, the prewar cars and the 220.

rear-seat passengers like a protective covering. These cars were preferred in many lands for official motorcades in which the guest could wave to the multitudes; only a few private individuals were in a position to keep a 300 D Cabriolet. In all, 708 of these grandiose cars were built between 1951 and 1962. Today fans must pay six-figure sums, sometimes more than five times the price of the car when it was new, for such a car.

Though these two cars would have sufficed to convince the world of Daimler-Benz's ability to excel, there was another reason to stop and stare at the Paris Auto Show in the autumn of 1951. On the basis of the Type 300, a two-seater with occasional seats had been developed and designated the 300 S, to be built in three versions as a coupe, convertible or roadster with lowering folded top. This dream car brought back memories of the legendary 540 K of the Thirties, one of the most beautiful cars of all time. The bodies of the new 300 S cars, with their dynamically sweeping fenders, very long motor hoods and long curving tails, gave an impression of powerful forward motion, along with exemplary elegance; a car that people stopped in their tracks to stare at when it glided by. To make the body, mounted on the shortened 300 chassis, move fast enough to meet expectations, the engineers of Daimler-Benz raised the motor's compression to 7.8:1 and turned fuel mixing over to three instead of two Solex downdraft carburetors. The impressive result added up to 150 HP at 5000 rpm, which let the car exceed 100 kph in barely more than 15 seconds and attain almost 180 kph, figures that, when production began in the summer of 1952, had been achieved by no production car in Germany.

After the coupe version, which could be had with a big folding convertible top that considerably heightened the charm of this car, the cabriolet was the most popular version. The huge chromed irons on the sides of its convertible top were striking, as was the tiny window slot in the back, which scarcely offered a sufficient view to the rear but looked very classy. Only very few of the roadster version were built; here the top disappeared completely under a sheet-metal flap behind the rear seats, making the car look particularly harmonious and spirited, especially from the side, since the top did not sit atop the rear of the car like a big bundle. Of course not many people could afford one of these cars, which was an outstanding example of car building in the early Fifties. Between 1951 and 1958 no fewer than 760 were built, and prices between 34,500 and 36,500 Marks made the two-seater a desirable plaything for movie stars, big businessmen and rich Americans.

In 1955 there were even a few improvements made to the 300 S, which was called the 300 Sc from then on and offered Bosch fuel injection and 8.58:1 compression, producing 175 HP. This motor was closely related to the 215 HP powerplant of the 300 SL sports car, and moved the 300 Sc, which weighed almost two tons, remarkably easily. Only 200 such cars were produced and equipped with power steering and swing axle.

But the Type 300 sedan also underwent numerous important changes and improvements during its eleven-year life. In March of 1954, a reworked Mercedes known as the 300 b was introduced; with its compression raised to 7.5:1 and two-stage Solex carburetion, it produced 10 HP more than its predecessor. To activate the second stage of carburetion, one had to apply a higher pedal pressure. The car was elastic enough so that one could accelerate in high gear anywhere above 20 kph without straining the engine. The brake system of the first 300, which

was perhaps a bit undersized, had its brake surface enlarged by approximately 200 cc, whereupon the car stopped safely without fading, even under hard braking.

In September of 1955 this 300 b was replaced by the 300 c, externally recognizable by its considerably enlarged rear end. From this model on, the rear wheels were driven by a single-link swing axle, and whoever wanted solid comfort could now obtain the 300 c with a three-speed Borg-Warner automatic transmission built under license. This cost the car some 5 kph in terms of top speed, but this was no great problem in terms of the car's fine performance. For special occasions, the 300 c was available as of the summer of 1956 with a wheelbase lengthened by 20cm, jump seats in the back and an electrically lowering glass panel behind the front seats. Some of these cars, measuring a good 5.16 meters in length, were equipped with short-wave telephones—at that time a huge apparatus that took up a lot of space in the front—for government use.

At the end of 1957, when all other Mercedes-Benz cars had had their separate chassis replaced by a modern self-bearing body, the classic 300 again underwent major improvements. The engine performance took another step upward to 160 HP with the installation of Bosch fuel injection, and noticeable redesigning had taken place externally as well. The car was now called a "Hardtop Limousine", for all the side windows, including frames, could now be lowered. The wheelbase had grown by 10cm, and the luggage space between the newly reshaped, more angular fenders had grown much larger. It was ideal for the set of suitcases made especially for this car and sold by the factory, as was also done for other models including the 300 S. Safety controls and a light flasher connected to the horn completed the already lavish equipment of the car, which was so highly developed as to leave as good as nothing to be wished for.

By 1962, 3207 of this classic Mercedes had been made, with the successor Type 300 SE already available in its last production year. This very different, smaller new 300 car, with its modern monocoque construction, was considerably less expensive and time-consuming to build, and its comparatively simple styling suited a wider circle of customers than the mighty "flagship." Besides that, the developmental section of Daimler-Benz was preparing another sensation in car building in the form of the Type 600.

The "Adenauer-Mercedes", as it was called on account of its most prominent user, wrote a chapter of automotive history. When its production ended, the greater part of those stylistic influences that had survived at Daimler-Benz from the Thirties, and from the unforgettable prestige cars made then, disappeared. Surviving old 300s—and there are quite a number of them—are either lovingly and lavishly restored to their original condition or still driven, maintained and preserved by their first or second owners; automotive classics of this type will not be forgotten.

Luggage was available to fit the 300 sedan or convertible.

Respect for Superlatives

At the first International Automobile Exposition held in Frankfurt after the war, an international-class prestige car made its debut—the Type 300 by Mercedes-Benz. The impressive styling of the heavy body, along with a powerful motor, soon made this car the preferred vehicle for politicians inside and outside Germany. More than ten years were to pass before a replacement for this classic prestige car was needed.

The famous graphic artist **Walter Gotschke** created the dynamic illustrations for the first 300 catalog.

Typ 300

C A B R I O L E T "D"

Typ 300

Typ 300
CABRIOLET "D"

The motor, based on new technology with many new and progressive features, offers an optimum of performance, quiet running and long life. Thermostatically regulated cooling and lubricating oil circulation result in quick and even warming when the engine starts, additional cylinder lubrication after starting, thermostatically regulated oil temperature, two Solex downdraft carburetors with three-duct system and accelerator pump, air intake via a sound damper and automatically regulated air-duct heating, a distributor with octane-count compensator, 12-volt generator and many other signs of high technical development characterize this powerful motor. Its great elasticity and high range of engine speed guarantee easy and yet spirited driving, almost without shifting, in any traffic conditions, and speeds of up to 115 kph on the Autobahn.

For the front wheels, the independent suspension with parallel transverse links, already proved on Mercedes-Benz racing cars, was chosen. Soft, friction-free coil springs with large spring lengths, rubber auxiliary springs, and telescopic shock absorbers located inside the coil springs provide for secure road-handling and excellent suspension, even at high speed on rough roads. The whole suspension system is attached to the frame via rubber bushings.

The precise, soft and jerk-free Mercedes-Benz steering was developed for the special requirements of this fast car. It is practically play-free and maintains this condition constantly as a result of its automatic adjustment. A hydraulic brake system prevents the steering from jerking, even on the roughest roads.

The proved Mercedes-Benz swing axle, with independently mounted and sprung wheels, serves as the rear axle of this car too. Power transmission takes place via the hypoid gearing first developed in Germany and operates fully noiselessly. Suspension is provided by soft, friction-free coil springs with auxiliary springing and telescopic shock absorbers here too. The auxiliary suspension can be turned on or off, according to the load in the car, from the driver's seat. This system was used for the first time in this car, thus providing the same outstanding suspension and road-handling for any load. Through the careful tuning of the front and rear suspensions, the wheels' inclination to toe in horizontally and

Right: Even more elegant than the sedan was the 5- or 6-passenger Cabriolet D.

Below: With a top speed of 155 kph, the 300 was King of the Autobahn in the early Fifties.

Der nach neuen Erkenntnissen mit vielen neuen fortschrittlichen Konstruktionsideen geschaffene Motor bietet ein Optimum

an Leistung, Laufruhe und Lebensdauer. Thermostatisch regulierter Kühlmittel- und Schmierölumlauf ergibt rasche und gleichmäßige Start-Erwärmung, Zylinder-Zusatzschmierung nach dem Start, thermostatisch regulierte Temperatur des Schmieröls, zwei Solex-Fallstromvergaser mit Dreidüsensystem und Beschleunigerpumpe, Luftansaugung über Geräuschdämpfer und automatisch regulierte Saugrohrvorwärmung, Zündverteiler mit Oktanzahlkompensator, 12-Volt-Lichtanlage und viele andere Merkmale hoher technischer Vollendung kennzeichnen diesen kraftvollen Motor. Seine große Elastizität und hohe Drehzahlspanne gestatten ein fast schaltungsfreies weiches und doch äußerst temperamentvolles Fahren bei

allen Verkehrsbedingungen, auf der Autobahn Geschwindigkeiten von gestoppten ca. 155 Stundenkilometern.

Für die Vorderräder wurde die schon bei den Mercedes-Benz-Rennwagen bewährte Einzelrad-Aufhängung mit Parallel-Querlenkern gewählt. Weiche reibungsfreie Schraubenfedern mit großen Federwegen, Gummi-Zusatzfedern und im Innern der Schraubenfedern angeordnete Teleskop-Stoßdämpfer sorgen für eine sichere Straßenlage und hervorragende Federung auch auf schlechtesten Straßen bei voller Geschwindigkeit. Das ganze Federungssystem ist in Gummi gegen den Rahmen gelagert.

Die präzise, weiche und stoßfreie Mercedes-Benz-Lenkung wurde den besonderen Erfordernissen dieses schnellen Wagens entsprechend ausgebildet. Sie ist praktisch spielfrei und behält diesen

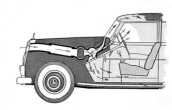

Zustand auch dauernd infolge der automatischen Nachstellung

bei. Eine hydraulische Bremseinrichtung verhindert auch bei schlechtesten Straßen ein Schlagen der Lenkung.

Als Hinterachse dient auch bei diesem Typ die bewährte Mercedes-Benz-Pendelachse mit einzeln abgefederten und abgestützten Rädern. Die Kraftübertragung erfolgt durch die erstmals in Deutschland verwendete Hypoidverzahnung und arbeitet

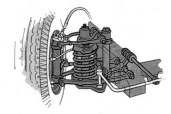

völlig geräuschlos. Zur Abfederung dienen auch hier weiche reibungslose Schraubenfedern mit einer Zusatzfederung und Teleskop-Stoßdämpfern. Die Zusatzfederung kann je nach der Belastung des Wagens vom Fahrersitz zu-oder abgeschaltet werden. Diese Anordnung wurde bei diesem Fahrzeug erstmalig angewandt und ergibt damit für jeden Belastungsfall die gleiche ausgezeichnete Federung und Straßenlage. Durch die sorgfältige Abstimmung des Federungs-Systems der Vorder- und Hinterräder, die Nachgiebigkeit der Räder in horizontaler Richtung und

14

he particularly large speedometer is
mounted high up in the driver's direct
field of vision, so that the driver does not
need to take his eyes off the road to read
. The brightness of the instrument
lighting can be regulated as desired.
Three different-colored warning lights
in the dashboard indicate the settings of
the directional signals, the starter and
the high-beam headlights. The other
operating controls too, as well as the
ashtray and cigarette lighter, are close at
hand and easy to see. A radio set with
automatic station selection can be
mounted in the dashboard optionally.
The beautifully formed rear of the car,
with its strong bumper and the directional lights that are insensitive to the
effect of other light, contains a large
luggage space; the spare wheel is also
housed in it. The light for the license
plate, which is mounted on the trunk
lid, also serves to illuminate the trunk.
Three people can sit comfortably on the
front and the rear seat. The front seats
are easy to adjust for comfort and driving
safety in terms of both direction and the
inclination of the seat back, but can also
be turned into a bench. The handy
steering-column shifting of the fully
synchronized four-speed transmission
gives the occupants of the front seats full
foot space. The two-spoke steering wheel
holds the well-known Mercedes horn
ring, which simultaneously serves to
turn the directional signals on and off.
The front and rear seats have armrests at
the sides, and the rear seat also has a
folding central armrest. To make getting
in and out easier, handholds with
folding coat hooks are mounted above
the windows. Behind the rear seats there
is a roomy storage area. The rear-view
mirror has a special non-glare setting,
so that at night the view through the
large rear window can be observed
without glare. The bowed windshield
offers the driver an excellent view.
Cranked windows are built into all the
doors. A large glove compartment with
a locking cover on the dashboard, as
well as roomy pockets on the doors,
provide for storage or small items.

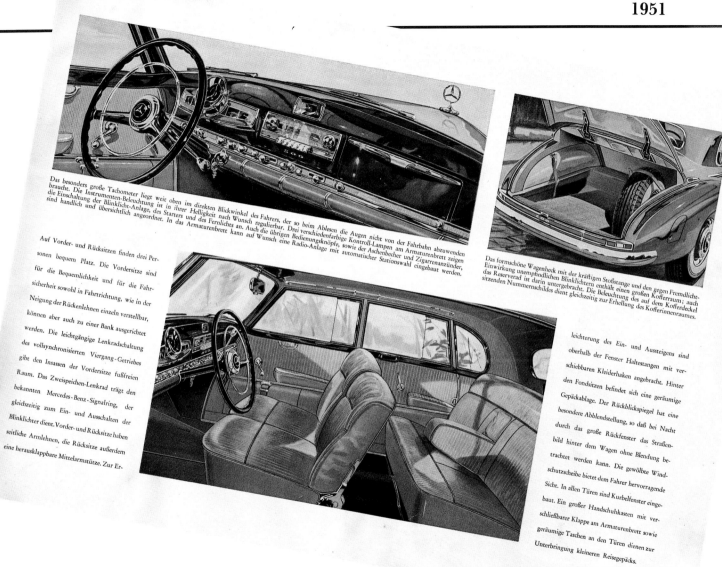

Das besonders große Tachometer liegt weit oben im direkten Blickwinkel des Fahrers, der so beim Ablesen die Augen nicht von der Fahrbahn abzuwenden braucht. Die Instrumenten-Beleuchtung ist in ihrer Helligkeit nach Wunsch regulierbar. Drei verschiedenfarbige Kontroll-Lampen am Armaturenbrett zeigen die Einschaltung der Blinklicht-Anlage, des Starters und des Fernlichts an. Auch die übrigen Bedienungsknöpfe, sowie der Aschenbecher und Zigarrenanzünder, sind handlich und übersichtlich angeordnet. In das Armaturenbrett kann auf Wunsch eine Radio-Anlage mit automatischer Stationswahl eingebaut werden.

Das formschöne Wagenheck mit der kräftigen Stoßstange und den gegen Fremdlicht-Einwirkung unempfindlichen Blinklichtern enthält einen großen Kofferraum; auch das Reserverad ist darin untergebracht. Die Beleuchtung des auf dem Kofferdeckel sitzenden Nummernschildes dient gleichzeitig zur Erhellung des Kofferinnenraumes.

Auf Vorder- und Rücksitzen finden drei Personen bequem Platz. Die Vordersitze sind für die Bequemlichkeit und für die Fahrsicherheit sowohl in Fahrtrichtung, wie in der Neigung der Rückenlehnen einzeln verstellbar, können aber auch zu einer Bank ausgerichtet werden. Die leichtgängige Lenkradschaltung des vollsynchronisierten Viergang-Getriebes gibt den Insassen der Vordersitze fußfreien Raum. Das Zweispeichen-Lenkrad trägt den bekannten Mercedes-Benz-Signalring, der gleichzeitig zum Ein- und Ausschalten der Blinklichter dient. Vorder- und Rücksitze haben seitliche Armlehnen, die Rücksitze außerdem eine herausklappbare Mittelarmstütze. Zur Er-

leichterung des Ein- und Aussteigens sind oberhalb der Fenster Haltestangen mit verschiebbaren Kleiderhaken angebracht. Hinter den Fondsitzen befindet sich eine geräumige Gepäckablage. Der Rückblickspiegel hat eine besondere Abblendstellung, so daß bei Nacht durch das große Rückfenster das Straßenbild hinter dem Wagen ohne Blendung betrachtet werden kann. Die gewölbte Windschutzscheibe bietet dem Fahrer hervorragende Sicht. In allen Türen sind Kurbelfenster eingebaut. Ein großer Handschuhkasten mit verschließbarer Klappe am Armaturenbrett sowie geräumige Taschen an den Türen dienen zur Unterbringung kleineren Reisegepäcks.

**Above: Naturally the most luxurious atmosphere prevailed
in the interior too, thanks to the finest materials and the
best workmanship.**

Below: the heavy body was borne by a solid chassis, and the suspension was very comfortable.

die selbst nachstellende Lenkung besitzt der „Typ 300" eine einzigartige Straßenlage und eine unwahrscheinlich große Reisegeschwindigkeit.

Lüftung und Heizung sind bei diesem Wagen zu besonders hoher Vollkommenheit entwickelt. Reine Luft wird über dem Kühler aufgefangen und einem Wärmetauscher zugeleitet, von dort in das Wageninnere geführt und über den ganzen Fußraum, die Windschutzscheibe sowie die vorderen Seitenscheiben verteilt. Damit hat der Fahrer auch nach den Seiten immer klare Sicht, wodurch die Fahrsicherheit bedeutend erhöht wird. Der Warm-

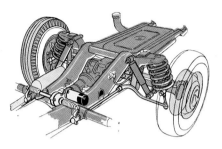

luftstrom kann auch ausschließlich zu der Windschutzscheibe und zu den beiden vorderen Seitenscheiben geführt werden, sobald Entfrostung notwendig ist. Zwei zusätzliche Gebläse sichern

Heizung und Entfrostung auch im Stand oder bei langsamer Geschwindigkeit des Wagens. Luftmenge und Temperatur können je nach Wunsch in feiner Abstimmung reguliert werden. Die Einstellung der Luftmenge geschieht durch zwei für rechts und links getrennte Regulierknöpfe, die Temperaturregelung durch einen in der Mitte angebrachten Drehknopf, mit dem über ein Wasserdrosselventil der gewünschte Wärmegrad eingestellt werden kann. Diese Kombination von Luftmengen- und Wärmeregulierung wirkt wie eine Klima-Anlage und fördert Sommer wie Winter das Wohlbefinden der Insassen auch auf langen Reisen.

The self-adjusting steering gives the "Type 300" unique road-handling capabilities and a surprisingly high cruising speed. Ventilation and heating have been developed to a particularly high level in this car. Fresh air is inducted via the radiator grille and conducted to a heat exchanger, from which it is ducted into the interior of the car and divided over the entire foot space, the windshield and the forward side windows. Thus the driver always has a clear view, including to the sides, which increases driving safety considerably. The stream of warm air can also be directed exclusively onto the windshield and the two forward side windows whenever defrosting is necessary. Two auxiliary blowers assure heating and defrosting, even when the car is standing still or moving slowly. The quantity and temperature of air can be regulated precisely as desired. The air adjustment is done by two separate controls at the right and left, and the temperature regulation by a control in the center, by which the desired degree of warmth can be set by means of a water-throttle valve. This combination of regulating the amount and warmth of air has the effect of air conditioning and assures the comfort of the passengers in winter and summer alike, even on long trips.

Two pictures provided by the factory for journalists to publish. Naturally, such a car made the best impression before a majestic background.

17

In such a car, the rear-seat passengers did not have to complain about a lack of freedom of movement; they had plenty of knee space, and softly upholstered armrests added to their comfort.

The individual front seat could be adjusted for any stature. The gigantic steering wheel was reminiscent of truck cabs but made steering easier.

Above: With a weight of 1.8 tons, the 300 was easily the heaviest passenger car made in Germany.

Right: Small items could be carried neatly in the easily opening door pockets.

MERCEDES-BENZ

Typ 300
noch schneller und wirtschaftlicher mit mehr Komfort

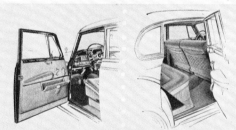

Die 4 großen, ganz mit Stoff belegten Wagentüren sind mit je einer gepolsterten Armlehne und geräumigen Seitentasche ausgestattet. An den Vordersitzrückwänden sind 2 Manteltaue und Netze für kleineres Handgepäck angebracht.

Dank seinem auf 125 PS erhöhten Motor, der dem „Typ 300" ein noch rasanteres Anzugsvermögen bis zur Spitzengeschwindigkeit von 160 km/std gibt, und der Steigerung von Sicherheit und Komfort wird dieses Fahrzeug zu einer eindruckvollen Höchstleistung. Der behagliche, große Innenraum, in dem 6 Personen bequem Platz haben, läßt auch bei langen Fahrten und hohen Reisedurchschnitten keine Ermüdung empfinden. Auch anspruchsvolle Wünsche nach Behaglichkeit und Eleganz sind erfüllt: 2 Einzelsitze vorne mit Ruhesitzeinrichtung oder eine durchgehende Sitzbank, in Längsrichtung verstellbar – hintere Sitze mit herausklappbarer mittlerer Armlehne – rechts und links oberhalb der Fenster durchgehende Haltestangen mit Kleiderhaken – 2 Innenleuchten – Armaturenbrett ganz aus poliertem Holz mit Kombi-Instrument im direkten Blickfeld des Fahrers – großer Handschuhkasten mit automatischer Innenbeleuchtung, dessen Klappe als Tischchen ausgebildet ist – abblendbarer Rückblickspiegel – Beleuchtung des Zigarrenanzünders und der Betätigungsknöpfe für Lüftung und Heizung – drehbare Belüftungsfenster an den Vordertüren – 2 Sonnenblenden, die rechte auf der Rückseite mit Spiegel – 2 Scheibenwischer mit überschneidendem Wischfeld und zwei Geschwindigkeiten – 3 Aschenbecher, einer im Armaturenbrett und zwei im Fond.

MERCEDES-BENZ Type 300
even faster and more economical with more comfort

The four large car doors, completely covered with cloth, are each provided with an upholstered armrest and a roomy side pocket. Two coat hooks and nets for small hand luggage are provided on the backs of the front seats.
Thanks to its motor, upgraded to 125 HP, the "Type 300" is able to accelerate to its top speed of 160 kph even more quickly, and with increased safety and comfort, this car achieves impressively high performance. The comfortable, spacious interior, in which six persons can sit in comfort, causes no weariness, even on long drives or frequent trips. High standards of comfort and elegance are also fulfilled: two individual front seats with seat-back adjustment or a complete seat bench, adjustable longitudinally—back seats with a folding central armrest—extensive handholds over the windows, with coat hooks—two interior lights—dashboard completely made of polished wood with combined instruments in the driver's direct field of vision—a large glove compartment with automatic interior lighting and a lid that is designed to serve as a small table—glare-free rear-view mirror—lighting for the cigarette lighter and the control knobs for ventilation and heating—adjustable vent windows in the front doors—two sun visors, the right one with a mirror on the back—two windshield wipers with overlapping wiping fields and two speeds—three ashtrays, one in the dashboard and two in the rear.

Schneller Der 6-Zylinder-Hochleistungs-motor des „Typ 300" besitzt eine große Elastizität und Laufruhe, die durch seine Drehzahlfestigkeit bis 6000 U/min in Verbindung mit 2 neuen Mehrstufenvergasern erreicht wurde. Damit und durch die Erhöhung des Verdichtungsverhältnisses auf 1:7,5 ist eine Leistungssteigerung erzielt, die der Verstärkung des Drehmomentes vor allem im unteren und mittleren Drehzahlbereich zugute kommt. Bei einer Erhöhung der Spitzengeschwindigkeit auf 160 km/std konnten so Beschleunigung und Bergsteigevermögen des Mercedes-Benz „Typ 300" beträchtlich verbessert werden.

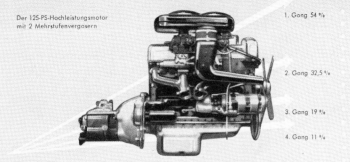

Der 125-PS-Hochleistungsmotor mit 2 Mehrstufenvergasern

1. Gang 54 %

2. Gang 32,5 %

3. Gang 19 %

4. Gang 11 %

Wirtschaftlicher Zu den technischen Verbesserungen kommt eine Erhöhung der Wirtschaftlichkeit, die auf eine rationellere Gemischbildung der Mehrstufenvergaser zurückzuführen ist. Während bei geringer Leistungsanforderung und bei niederer Drehzahl grundsätzlich nur jeweils eine Stufe eingeschaltet ist, wird bei höherem Kraftbedarf eine zweite Stufe automatisch zugeschaltet. Eine automatische Startvorrichtung macht die übliche von Hand zu bedienende Luftklappe überflüssig.

Öldruckbremse mit Unterdruckverstärkung

Bremstrommeln mit Turbokühlung

Sicherer Der erhöhten Leistung steht eine Steigerung der Fahrsicherheit gegenüber. Die Wirkung der turbogekühlten Öldruckbremse wurde zusätzlich durch Unterdruck verstärkt. Das vom Rennsportwagen „Typ 300 SL" übernommene Bremsaggregat gibt auch bei übermäßiger, langanhaltender Beanspruchung durch seine großdimensionierten Leichtmetall-Perlitguß-Bremstrommeln mit Turbokühlung höchste Sicherheit.

TECHNISCHE DATEN

Zylinderzahl	6
Bohrung/Hub	85/88 mm
Gesamthubraum effektiv	2996 ccm
Verdichtungsverhältnis	1:7,5
Oktanzahl des Kraftstoffs	Tankstellenkraftstoff mit mindestens 78 Oktan nach Motor-Methode (z. B. Superkraftstoffe)
Drehzahl bei 100 km/std	3570 U/min
Höchstdrehzahl	6000 U/min
Motorleistung*	125 PS/4500 U/min (SAE 136 HP)
Kraftstoffnormverbrauch**	12,5 Ltr./100 km
Tankinhalt	72 Ltr.
davon Reserve	6 Ltr.
Inhalt der Kühlanlage mit Heizung	ca. 20 Ltr.
Ölfüllung des Kurbelgehäuses, max.	6,5 Ltr.
min.	4 Ltr.
Höchstgeschwindigkeit	
1. Gang	45 km/std
2. Gang	68 km/std
3. Gang	111 km/std
4. Gang	ca. 160 km/std
Reifengröße	7,10-15; 6 Lagen
Batteriekapazität	12 V/70 Ah
Größte Länge des Fahrzeugs	5055 mm
Größte Breite des Fahrzeugs	1838 mm
Größte Höhe des Fahrzeugs unbelastet	1600 mm
Radstand	3050 mm
Spurweite vorn	1480 mm
Spurweite hinten	1525 mm
Bodenfreiheit, mit 2 Personen besetzt	215 mm
Wendekreis-Durchmesser	ca. 12,6 m
Fahrzeuggewicht fahrfertig	1770 kg

* Die angegebene Leistung in PS ist nach Abzug aller Nebenleistungen an der Kupplung für den Antrieb des Wagens effektiv verfügbar.

** Ermittelt bei ⅔ der Höchstgeschwindigkeit unter Zuschlag von 10 %.

Lt. VDA-Revers technische Angaben entsprechend DIN 70 020 und 70 030.

Änderungen in Konstruktion und Ausstattung vorbehalten.

ÄLTESTE AUTOMOBILFABRIK DER WELT

DAIMLER - BENZ AKTIENGESELLSCHAFT STUTTGART - UNTERTÜRKHEIM

Printed in Germany III. 54. 50. F

In March of 1954 the Type 300 b appeared, with its performance upgraded by 10 HP and its braking system adapted from the 300 SL sports car.

One of the most beautiful and elegant vehicles of the postwar era was and is the Cabriolet D, the open version of the Mercedes-Benz 300. Carefully, laboriously handcrafted, only 708 of these cars, now almost impossible to obtain, were produced during its production time. The huge, yet very precisely raised and lowered top was itself a masterpiece of skilled handiwork, and a drive in such a car ranks among the most impressive of experiences for a lover of classic cars.

Whether its top was up or down, the Cabriolet D made an impressively beautiful appearance. Lower left: When it was down, the folded top made a bundle that one could scarcely see beyond.

Expensive fabrics or leather and the lavish use of hardwood veneer made one's stay in the Type 300 comfortable and stylish.

Safety and complete driving comfo[rt] most important demands on a moder[n] mobile—go without saying for the ow[ner of] the Mercedes-Benz. This is owed to the [wealth] of experience of the world's oldest auto[mobile] factory, whose progressive develop[ment] work has been directed from the start [by the] basic concepts of the greatest safety. [So] designs originated that have been deci[sive for] the outstanding road-handling and [high] driving safety of all Mercedes-Benz ve[hicles]. The characteristics and construction o[f these] perfected cars are now, more than ever [a] part of the proverbial concept of "Me[rcedes-] Benz safety." They are also the requi[site] for the success of the internationally a[dmired] Type 300.

One enters easily and unimpeded th[rough] the four doors, whose hinges are loca[ted at] the front. The costly fabric upho[lstery] divided by polished wooden panels, the [large] opening pockets and upholstered ar[mrests] on the doors, the folding central arm[rest in] the back, the coat hooks and luggage n[ets on] the back of the front seats, and ple[nty of] handholds with coat hooks over the [side] windows are a few examples of ma[nifold] comfort.

You can choose as you wish betwee[n] individual front seats with adjustable [backs] and a seat bench whose back is lik[ewise] adjustable.

The front seat bench can be equi[pped] optionally with a comfortable folding [arm] rest.

To further increase your comfort on [long] drives, a headrest can be obtained optio[nally] for individual seats.

Je nach Wunsch kann zwischen zwei vorderen Einzelsitzen mit verstellbarer Rückenlehne und einer Sitzbank gewählt werden, deren Lehne ebenfalls verstellbar ist.

Die vordere Sitzbank kann auf Sonderwunsch mit einer herausklappbaren, behaglichen Armlehne versehen werden.

Zur weiteren Steigerung der Bequemlichkeit bei großer Fahrt, wird auf Sonderwunsch bei einzelsitzen eine Kopfstütze geliefert.

As of September 1955, one could also have an American Borg-Warner automatic transmission built in optionally. With its three gears, it naturally cost a bit of performance but spared the driver some work.

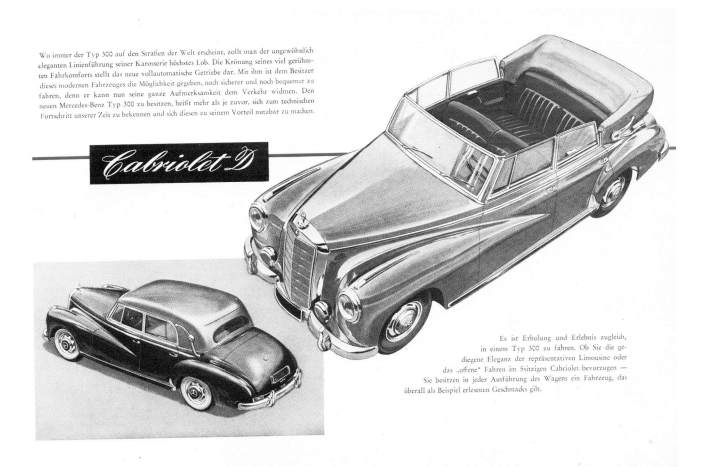

Wo immer der Typ 300 auf den Straßen der Welt erscheint, zollt man der ungewöhnlich eleganten Linienführung seiner Karosserie höchstes Lob. Die Krönung seines viel gerühmten Fahrkomforts stellt das neue vollautomatische Getriebe dar. Mit ihm ist dem Besitzer dieses modernen Fahrzeuges die Möglichkeit gegeben, noch sicherer und noch bequemer zu fahren, denn er kann nun seine ganze Aufmerksamkeit dem Verkehr widmen. Den neuen Mercedes-Benz Typ 300 zu besitzen, heißt mehr als je zuvor, sich zum technischen Fortschritt unserer Zeit zu bekennen und sich diesen zu seinem Vorteil nutzbar zu machen.

Cabriolet D

Wherever the Type 300 appears on the world's roads, the unusually elegant styling of its body wins the highest praise. The finishing touch to its renowned driving comfort is provided by the new fully automatic transmission. With it, the owner of this modern car is able to drive even more safely and comfortably, for he can now devote his whole attention to the traffic. Owning the new Mercedes-Benz Type 300 means, more than ever before, recognizing the technical progress of our times and making use of it for one's benefit.

Cabriolet D

It is relaxation and enjoyment at the same time to ride in a Type 300. Whether you prefer the splendid elegance of the prestigious sedan or "open" driving in the five-seat cabriolet—in every version of the car you possess a vehicle that is recognized everywhere as an example of refined taste.

Es ist Erholung und Erlebnis zugleich, in einem Typ 300 zu fahren. Ob Sie die gediegene Eleganz der repräsentativen Limousine oder das „offene" Fahren im 5sitzigen Cabriolet bevorzugen — Sie besitzen in jeder Ausführung des Wagens ein Fahrzeug, das überall als Beispiel erlesenen Geschmacks gilt.

25

A feast for the eyes: the many chromed control knobs and switches on the dashboard, that require a conscientious study of the operator's manual.

Fahrkomfort, der Sicherheit bedeutet

Mit einem Blick erfaßt der Fahrer die ganze Fahrbahn; nach vorn durch die hohe, gewölbte Windschutzscheibe, nach rückwärts über den abblendbaren Rückblickspiegel durch das verbreiterte Heckfenster. In der großen Armaturentafel aus poliertem Holz sind die leicht ablesbaren Instrumente übersichtlich angeordnet, deren wichtigste in einem formschönen Kombi-Instrument zusammengefaßt sind. Hier hat der Fahrer Öldruckmesser, Kühlwasser-Temperaturmesser, Blinker-Kontrollampe, Tachometer mit Tageskilometerzähler, Amperemeter und den Drehknopf zur Regulierung der Lichtstärke der Instrumentenbeleuchtung direkt vor Augen.

Driving comfort that means safe

With one glance the driver takes i the whole roadway; to the fron through the high, bowed wind shield, to the rear via the glare-fre rear-view mirror through th widened rear window. In the larg instrument panel made of polishe wood, the easy-to-read instrumen are arranged handily, the mo important of them combined into beautifully formed combined in strument. Here the driver has th oil pressure gauge, water temp erature gauge, directional sign indicator, speedometer with dail odometer, ammeter and the kno that controls the brightness of th instrument lighting, all righ before his eyes.

Über die gewohnten Instrumente hinaus, wird für Fahrkomfort und Bedienung des Wagens geboten: Zugschalter für Deckenbeleuchtung · Schalter für Scheibenwischer mit 2 Geschwindigkeitsstufen · Drehschal-

ter für die elektrisch betätigte Zusatzfederung · Zugschalter für Dreiklang-Horn · Zigarrenanzünder · Oktanzahlkompensator · Hebel für getrennte Regulierung von Heizung und Lüftung für rechte und linke Wagenhälfte, von innen beleuchtet · Wählhebel für das automatische Getriebe mit Fahrskala oberhalb der Lenksäule · großer Handschuhkasten · Rückblickspiegel und eingebaute Leselampe

Raum und Komfort für große Reisen

Bequeme, weichgefederte Polstersitze mit besonders großzügig bemessenem Fußraum vor den Sitzen bieten 5 bis 6 Personen reichlich Platz. Für den Bezug wurden beim Innenlenker wertvolle Plüsch- oder Cordstoffe gewählt, während die Sitze des Cabriolets mit echtem Leder bezogen sind. Noch im kleinsten geschmackvollen Detail der Innenausstattung wird die Hand der erfahrenen Sindelfinger Karosseriebauer sichtbar, die in diesen repräsentativen Wagen alles einfügten, was dem Behagen seiner Insassen dient.

Der große Kofferraum im eleganten, langgezogenen Heck bietet ausgiebig Platz auch für umfangreiches Gepäck, für Reserverad und Werkzeug. Der verschließbare Deckel ist durch Druckfedern leicht zu heben und rastet in oberster Stellung selbst ein.

Das verbreiterte Heckfenster verbessert die Sicht auf die rückwärtige Fahrbahn und erhöht damit die Fahrsicherheit.

Das Reserverad ist rechts in einer Mulde stehend untergebracht und auch bei voller Beladung jederzeit zugänglich.

Geschmackvoll in einer Chromleiste angeordnet, liegen die kombinierten Schluß- und Bremsleuchten und der Rückfahrscheinwerfer.

Auf Sonderwunsch werden Koffersätze in drei verschiedenen Zusammenstellungen gegen Mehrpreis geliefert.

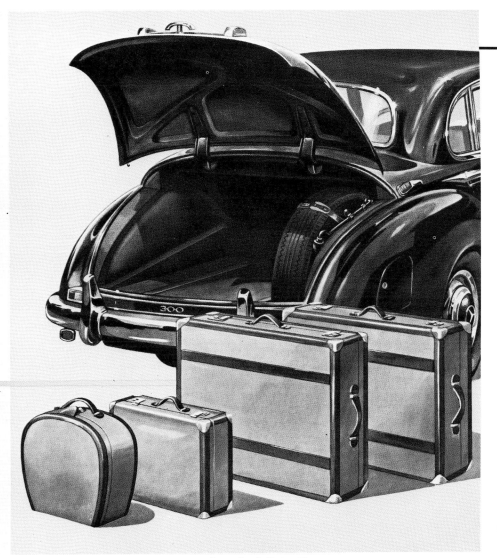

The 300 c version, built from 1955 on, is recognizable by its greatly enlarged rear window. For the large trunk of this car there was also a fitted set of luggage available.

Space and comfort for long trips

Comfortable, soft upholstered seats with particularly generous foot space in front of the seats offer five or six persons abundant space. For the interior upholstery, costly plush or corduroy fabrics were chosen, while the seats of the cabriolet are covered with genuine leather. Down to the smallest tasteful detail of the interior furnishing, the touch of the experienced Sindelfingen coachbuilder is apparent, which included in this prestigious car everything that serves the comfort of its passengers.

The large luggage compartment in the elegant, long-lined rear offers plentiful space for even considerable luggage, plus spare wheel and tools. The locking trunk lid is easy to raise, having pressure springs, and moves to its fully opened position automatically.

The widened rear window improves the view of the road in back and thus increases driving safety. The spare wheel is stored standing up in a well at the right side and is accessible at any time, even with the trunk fully loaded.

27

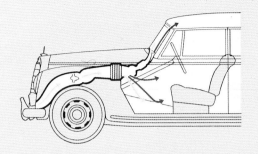

Wohlbehagen bei jeder Witterung

Wohltemperiert ist der Innenraum — bei jeder Witterung, im Winter wie im Sommer. Dafür sorgt die fein abstimmbare kombinierte Heizung und Lüftung. Durch Staudruck beim Fahren oder durch Gebläse im Stand angesaugt und durch zwei Wärmetauscher vorgewärmt, strömt die Luft, auf beiden Seiten getrennt regulierbar, in den Wagen. So können sowohl Fahrer als auch Beifahrer die Temperatur und Luftmenge ganz nach ihren Wünschen einstellen. Der Luftzustrom kann gesondert an die Windschutzscheibe und die Seitenscheiben geführt werden und sorgt im Winter für wirksame Entfrostung. Im Sommer schafft die sinnreich konstruierte Klima-Anlage eine angenehme, zugfreie Belüftung des ganzen Innenraumes des Wagens.

Comfort in any weather

The interior is "well-temperated" — in any storm, in winter as in summer. The finely adjustable combined heating and cooling takes care of that. Sucked in by pressure while driving or by blower when standing and then warmed by two heat exchanges, the air, regulated separately on each side, streams into the car. Thus the driver and passenger alike can regulate the temperature and amount of air just as they wish. The airstream can be directed specifically at the windshield and side windows, and provides effective defrosting in winter. In the summer the well-constructed air conditioning provides comfortable, draft-free ventilation of the whole interior of the car.

Despite the high degree of comfort, things taken for granted today, such as flashers and windshield washers were available only at extra charge then.

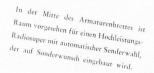

In der Mitte des Armaturenbrettes ist Raum vorgesehen für einen Hochleistungs-Radiosuper mit automatischer Senderwahl, der auf Sonderwunsch eingebaut wird.

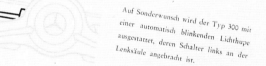

Auf Sonderwunsch wird der Typ 300 mit einer automatisch blinkenden Lichthupe ausgestattet, deren Schalter links an der Lenksäule angebracht ist.

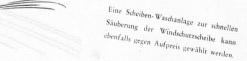

Eine Scheiben-Waschanlage zur schnellen Säuberung der Windschutzscheibe kann ebenfalls gegen Aufpreis gewählt werden.

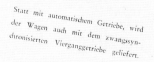

Statt mit automatischem Getriebe, wird der Wagen auch mit dem zwangssynchronisierten Vierganggetriebe geliefert.

In the middle of the dashboa... there is space provided for ... high-performance radio s... with automatic tuning, whic... can be built in optionally.

The Type 300 is optional... available with an aut... matically blinking lig... flasher, its switch located o... the left side of the steerin... column.

A windshield washer syster... for quick cleaning of th... windshield can likewise b... obtained at extra charge.

Instead of an automatic trans... mission, the car can also b... delivered with a fully synchro... nized four-speed gearbox.

Wherever the 300 appeared, it always drew
curious glances. Who might be getting out? 29

sche Getriebe

Einen zusätzlichen Schutz gegen das Rollen beim Halten im Verkehr bietet das automatische Anziehen der Bremsen, sobald der Wagen gestoppt wird. Sie können den Fuß vom Bremspedal nehmen und lösen im Augenblick des Anfahrens durch den Druck auf das Gaspedal automatisch die Bremsen. Zur Rückwärtsfahrt ist nur die Stellung des Wählhebels auf „R" und leichtes Gasgeben notwendig.

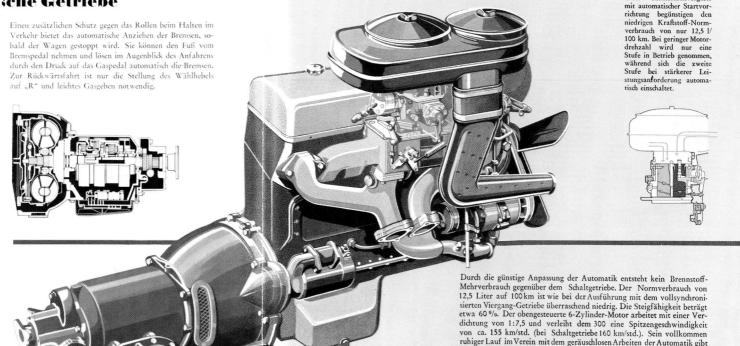

Zwei Mehrstufenvergaser mit automatischer Startvorrichtung begünstigen den niedrigen Kraftstoff-Normverbrauch von nur 12,5 l/100 km. Bei geringer Motordrehzahl wird nur eine Stufe in Betrieb genommen, während sich die zweite Stufe bei stärkerer Leistungsanforderung automatisch einschaltet.

Durch die günstige Anpassung der Automatik entsteht kein Brennstoff-Mehrverbrauch gegenüber dem Schaltgetriebe. Der Normverbrauch von 12,5 Liter auf 100 km ist wie bei der Ausführung mit dem vollsynchronisierten Viergang-Getriebe überraschend niedrig. Die Steigfähigkeit beträgt etwa 60 %. Der obengesteuerte 6-Zylinder-Motor arbeitet mit einer Verdichtung von 1:7,5 und verleiht dem 300 eine Spitzengeschwindigkeit von ca. 155 km/std. (bei Schaltgetriebe 160 km/std.). Sein vollkommen ruhiger Lauf im Verein mit dem geräuschlosen Arbeiten der Automatik gibt Zeugnis von dem idealen Zusammenwirken der hoch entwickelten Technik dieses Antriebsaggregats. Mehr als je zuvor können Sie die volle Kraft des 125-PS-Motors ausnützen, wo immer die Verkehrsverhältnisse es ermöglichen und vielleicht auch erfordern. Motor und Getriebe des neuen Typ 300 sind ein Beispiel für die außergewöhnlichen Leistungen, die die moderne Technik dem Automobilisten unserer Zeit bietet.

125 PS

The higher-compression motor of the 300 b, producing 125 HP, now let the car reach 160 kph and run a bit more smoothly.

Automatic Transmission

An additional protection against rolling while stopped in traffic is offered by the automatic activation of the brakes as soon as the car is stopped. You can take your foot off the brake pedal and the brakes will release at the moment of motion by the pressure on the gas pedal. To back up, only placing the lever in "R" and light pressure on the gas pedal are necessary.

Two multi-stage carburetors with automatic choke help achieve the low fuel consumption of only 12.5 liters per 100 km. At low engine speeds, only one stage is activated, while the second stage is activated automatically when higher performance is required.

Thanks to the favorable design of the automatic transmission, the fuel consumption is not higher than with a standard transmission. The consumption by norm of 12.5 liters per 100 km is as astonishingly low as with the fully synchronized four-speed transmission. The climbing ability amounts to about 60%. The overhead-cam 6-cylinder motor runs with a compression of 1:7.5 and gives the 300 a top speed of approximately 160 kph (with standard transmission, about 160 kph). Its completely quiet running, along with the soundless functioning of the automatic transmission, give evidence of the ideal cooperation of the highly developed technology of the powerplant aggregate. More than ever before, you can utilize the full power of the 125 HP motor wherever the traffic conditions allow it and perhaps even demand it. The motor and transmission of the new Type 300 are an example of the extraordinary performance that modern technology provides for the present-day motorist.

Das automatische Getriebe

Mit dem wahlweisen Einbau des vollautomatischen Getriebes im neuen 300 ist nicht nur der Wunsch vieler Automobilisten nach einer noch bequemeren Handhabung ihres Wagens verwirklicht. Hinter der Verfeinerung des Bedienungskomforts steht als wesentlicher Gewinn die Erhöhung der Fahrsicherheit. Besonders im dichten Großstadtverkehr bedeutet der Wegfall von Kuppeln und Schalten eine wesentliche Entlastung des Fahrers, der nun seine volle Aufmerksamkeit der Straße widmen kann. Ob Sie in voller Fahrt bremsen oder aus dem Stand plötzlich beschleunigen — immer genügt die Bedienung des Brems- oder Gaspedals. Die gesamten Schaltvorgänge werden von der mit idealen Abstimmungen arbeitenden Automatik übernommen. Dadurch wird das Fahren zügiger und die im normalen Verkehr oft unvermeidbare harte Beanspruchung von Motor und Getriebe völlig ausgeschaltet. Beim Parken (Stellung P) ist das gesamte Getriebe blockiert und damit jedes Rollen ausgeschlossen. Sie starten Ihren 300 in der Stellung „O" (Leergang) durch einen leichten Druck auf den Wählhebel in Richtung des Armaturenbretts. Zum Fahren auf normalen Strecken genügt es, wenn Sie den Hebel auf Normalfahrt (3) rücken. Diese Stellung kann praktisch immer beibehalten werden, ganz gleich, ob im Stadtverkehr mit zahlreichen Stops und sehr unterschiedlichen Geschwindigkeiten oder mit hohen Reisedurchschnitten auf Autobahnen gefahren wird. Bei jeder Geschwindigkeit von 0–155 km/std. ist hierbei automatisch die jeweils günstige Übersetzung eingeschaltet. An starken, langanhaltenden Steigungen, zum Beispiel bei Paßfahrten, ist die Stellung 1 einzuschalten. Bei steilen oder langen abfallenden Strecken ist sie ebenfalls zu benutzen und wirkt dabei als Motorbremse. Für starkes Beschleunigen wird das Gaspedal über die Vollgasstellung hinaus durchgetreten (Kickdown). Hierdurch wird je nach Geschwindigkeit der nächst niedrige Gang eingeschaltet und dieser in der Motordrehzahl voll ausgefahren.

Einen zusätzlichen Schutz gegen das Rollen beim Halten im Verkehr bietet das automatische Anziehen der Bremsen, sobald der Wagen gestoppt wird. Sie können den Fuß vom Bremspedal nehmen und lösen im Augenblick des Anfahrens durch den Druck auf das Gaspedal automatisch die Bremsen. Zur Rückwärtsfahrt ist nur die Stellung des Wählhebels auf „R" und leichtes Gasgeben notwendig.

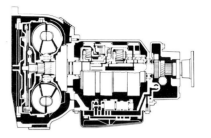

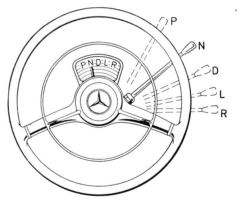

P = Park
N = Neutral
ST = Start
D a. L = Drive positions
R = Reverse

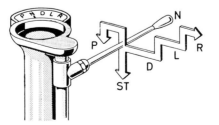

The automatic three-speed transmission, already common in America, was the height of luxury for German conditions, though even the use of the fully synchronized four-speed manual transmission caused no problems.

The Automatic Transmission
With the optional installation of the fully automatic transmission in the new 300, not only the wishes of many motorists for an even more convenient operation of the car are fulfilled. Beyond the refinement of operating convenience, there is noteworthy progress in the increase in driving safety. Especially in heavy city traffic, the absence of a need to declutch and shift provides an important unburdening for the driver, who can now devote his complete attention to the road conditions. Whether you brake while in motion or accelerate quickly from a stop—the use of the brake or gas pedal is always sufficient. The whole work of shifting is taken over by the ideally designed automatic transmission. Thus driving becomes smoother, and the hard use of the motor and gears, often unavoidable in normal driving, is fully eliminated. When parked (position P), the entire system is blocked and thus any rolling is prevented. You start your 300 in position "O" (neutral) by light pressure on the selector lever in the direction of the dashboard. For driving on normal roads it is sufficient for you to put the lever in the normal driving position (3). This setting can be maintained almost all the time, no matter whether you are driving in city traffic with many stops and at widely varying speeds, or on the superhighway at a high sustained speed. At any speed from zero to 155 kph, the most favorable transmission is activated at any time. For heavy, long-lasting acceleration, or when passing, position 1 should be chosen. It can also be used on steep upgrades or long downgrades and thus works as a brake on the engine. For heavy acceleration, the gas pedal is pushed beyond the usual full-gas position (kickdown). Thereby, according to the speed, the next lower gear is engaged and fully utilized at the engine speed.

An additional protection against rolling when stopped in traffic is offered by the automatic activation of the brakes as soon as the car is stopped. You can take your foot off the brake pedal and the pressure on the brakes is released automatically the moment you step on the gas. For driving in reverse, you need only move the indicator lever to "R" and press lightly on the gas pedal.

A noteworthy detail of the car's rear suspension was the auxiliary suspension, adjustable electrically from the driver's seat, that provided equalization when carrying a heavy load.

The play-free and automatically adjusting Mercedes-Benz rotating-ball steering stands out by its particularly light movement and outstanding contact with the roadbed. It is one of the many technical advantages of the Type 300, which add up to provide its outstanding driving comfort and subordinate the car's power and speed to the will of the driver.

Die spielfreie und automatisch nachstellende Mercedes-Benz Kugelumlauf-Lenkung zeichnet sich durch besondere Leichtgängigkeit und vorzüglichen Kontakt mit der Fahrbahn aus. Sie ist einer der vielen technischen Vorzüge des Typ 300, die zusammen seinen berühmten Fahrkomfort ergeben und die Kraft und Schnelligkeit dieses Wagens dem Willen des Fahrers unterordnen.

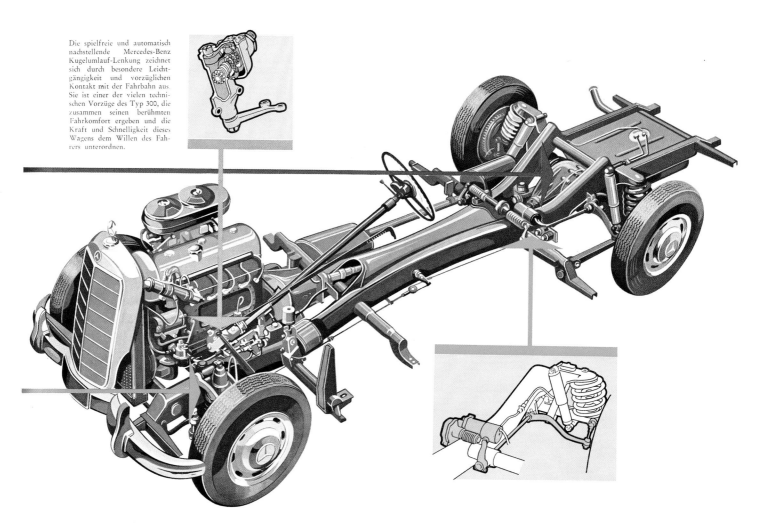

Grundlage Ihrer Sicherheit

Das Rückgrat des Typ 300 bildet ein äußerst stabiler, aus ovalen Längsträgern und eingeschweißten Rohr-Querträgern zusammengesetzter Rahmen. Seine Festigkeit, auch unter hoher Belastung und starker Beanspruchung auf Zug und Druck, ist die Grundlage der überragenden Sicherheit dieses Wagens. Der gesamte Aufbau ist mit dem Rahmen zu einer besonders widerstandsfähigen Einheit fest verschweißt.

In die Bodenanlage sind Motor, Getriebe und Achsen aufgenommen. Ihre Gummilagerung im Verein mit der Elastizität des Unterbaues ergeben eine vorzügliche Dämpfung aller Fahrbahnerschütterungen selbst auf ausgesprochen schlechten Straßen und bei schärfster Fahrweise. Durch den Einbau der Eingelenk-Pendelachse ist zudem die Bodenhaftung der Räder noch mehr verbessert worden, während die Zusatzfederung der Hinterräder die völlige Anpassung an die Gegebenheiten der Straßen ermöglicht. Das Resultat dieser sorgfältig durchdachten Rahmenanlage ist ein Höchstmaß an Schutz und Komfort für die Insassen, eine weitgehende Unabhängigkeit vom Straßenzustand bei jeder Fahrweise und die schon sprichwörtliche „Mercedes-Benz-Sicherheit", die in diesem Wagen eine überzeugende Ausprägung erfahren hat.

The Basis of Your Safety

The backbone of the Type 300 is formed by an extremely stable chassis composed of oval longitudinal members and welded-on tube transverse members. Its rigidity, even under heavy loads and heavy demands in terms of motion and pressure, is the basis of the outstanding safety of this car. The entire body is firmly welded to the chassis to form a particularly resistant unit.

At the bottom level, the motor, gearbox and axles are attached. Their rubber mountings along with the elasticity of the subframe provide outstanding dampening of all road-surface disturbance, even on remarkably rough roads and under the hardest driving. Through the use of the single-joint swing axle, the road-handling of the wheels has even been improved, while the auxiliary suspension of the rear wheels makes it possible to suit the suspension to the road conditions completely. The result of this carefully designed chassis is the highest degree of protection and comfort for the passengers, a considerable independence from road conditions in any type of driving, and the already proverbial "Mercedes-Benz safety" that has attained a convincing state of perfection in this car.

The mighty chassis, along with the heavy body, made it possible to maximize the comfort of the suspension in a way that made the 300 one of the most comfortable cars in the world, allowing one to undertake even the longest trips without any particular signs of weariness.

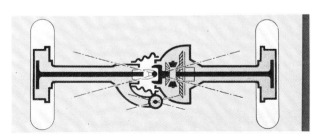

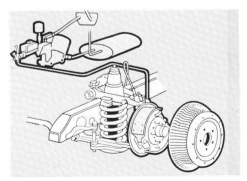

Even more exclusive than the 300 sedan was the 2+2-seat 300 S introduced only at the end of 1951. Optically as well as technically, this car could bring back memories of the glorious sports cars of the Twenties and Thirties. The 300 S had scarcely any competitors in terms of performance. Sale of the 300 S, though, began only in July of 1952.

52133

The 300-S
Cabriolet
depicted here
was only one of
the three body
types available.

Whoever was
allowed to enter
the luxurious
interior of this
dream car
through the
massive doors
had access to the
epitome of
German
automobile
construction.

Zeugnis meisterlichen Automobilbaues

Wenn es je gelungen ist, ein Automobil zu bauen, das den Stempel des Außergewöhnlichen in jedem Detail trägt, dann ist es der weltberühmte 300 S — der Wagen, der die stolze Serie der Fahrzeuge mit dem Mercedes-Benz-Stern anführt.

Es war das Ziel seiner Konstrukteure, ein Fahrzeug zu schaffen, das in seinen Fahreigenschaften und seiner Motorleistung, seiner Schönheit und seiner luxuriösen Innenausstattung beispielhaft sein sollte für den hohen Stand modernen Automobilbaues. Es sollte aber, traditionellem Mercedes-Benz-Grundsatz gemäß, auch ein echtes Gebrauchsfahrzeug sein, das seinem Besitzer in allen Verkehrssituationen und auf jeder Fahrt vollkommene Sicherheit bietet. Der Stolz der 300 S-Besitzer und die Bewunderung der Automobilexperten in aller Welt haben bewiesen, daß Mercedes-Benz dieses Ziel erreichte: der 300 S ist zum absoluten Maßstab seiner Klasse geworden. In seiner neuen Ausführung mit dem kraftvollen Einspritzmotor nach dem Vorbild des 300 SL ist er mehr denn je Sinnbild für die ideale Vereinigung von Sportlichkeit und Komfort, von überragender Schnelligkeit und edler Schönheit.

Cabriolet A **Ein Wagen für Verwöhnte**

Right: Somewhat less daring personalities chose the weathertight coupe, and whoever wanted to be thoroughly sporting could pay 34,500 DM for the roadster, whose folded top disappeared under a sheet metal cover.

Guarantee of Masterful Car Building

If it has ever been possible to build an automobile that bears the stamp of the extraordinary in every detail, then it is the world-famous 300 S—the car that leads the proud parade of vehicles with the Mercedes-Benz star.

It was the goal of its designers to create a vehicle that was to be an example of the high level of modern automobile construction in terms of its handling characteristics and engine performance, its beauty and its luxurious interior furnishings. Yet according to traditional Mercedes-Benz principles, it was to be a genuinely useful car as well, which offers its possessor complete safety in all driving situations and on every trip. The pride of the 300 S owner and the admiration of automotive experts all over the world have proved that Mercedes-Benz has attained this goal: the 300 S has become the absolute standard for its class. In its new version, with its powerful fuel-injection motor that follows the example of the 300 SL, it is more than ever the model of the ideal unification of sportiness and comfort, overwhelming speed and noble beauty.

Cabriolet A—A Car for the Pampered

Coupé

Für Autokenner

mit individuellem Geschmack

Coupe for connoisseurs with individual taste
Roadster: comfort and sportiness united.

Komfort und Sportlichkeit vereint

Roadster

Luxuriöse Bequemlichkeit

Was die Eleganz der äußeren Linien des 300 S verspricht, erfüllt sich in der einzigartigen Bequemlichkeit des großen Innenraumes. Erlesenes Material und seine meisterliche Verarbeitung schaffen eine Atmosphäre gepflegter Behaglichkeit, in der die Insassen den Komfort der weichen, lederbezogenen Sitze und die vielen Annehmlichkeiten der Ausstattung voll genießen können. Von den matt glänzenden Edelholzleisten über die wertvollen Leder- und Stoffbezüge bis zu den verchromten Griffen und Beschlägen ist alles nicht nur wohltuend für das Auge, sondern auch im Hinblick auf sinnvolle Zweckmäßigkeit durchdacht. Das Resultat ist eine Bequemlichkeit, die auch für Anspruchsvolle nichts zu wünschen übrigläßt.

Luxurious comfort
What the elegance of the external lines of the 300 S promises is fulfilled in the unique comfort of the spacious interior. Choice materials and their masterful tailoring create an atmosphere of cultivated comfort in which the passengers can fully enjoy the comfort of the soft leather-covered seats and the many amenities of the furnishings. From the glistening matte finish of the hardwood paneling over the costly leather and cloth upholstery to the chromed handles and trim, everything is not only a treat for the eye, but also designed with an eye to sensible practicality. The result is comfort that leaves nothing to be desired, even for those who demand the best.

Two wide chromed frames, designed to harmonize with the form of the car at the rear, house the combined tail- and brake lights, directional lights and back-up light.

Praktische Eleganz

Das langgezogene, elegant geschwungene Heck umschließt einen großen Kofferraum. Ohne Verzicht auf den harmonischen Fluß der äußeren Linien ist hier Platz für zwei große Spezialkoffer geschaffen worden. Der breite Deckel läßt sich dank der eingebauten Ausgleichsfedern mühelos anheben und rastet in oberster Stellung selbsttätig ein. Gleichzeitig schaltet sich automatisch die Kofferraumbeleuchtung ein. Das Reserve-Rad ist rechts stehend untergebracht und auch bei voller Beladung jederzeit leicht zugänglich. Auf Sonderwunsch wird ein weiteres Reserve-Rad geliefert, das in einer — serienmäßig mit Abdeckung versehenen — zweiten Mulde seitlich links untergebracht werden kann. Zur Normalausstattung gehören die beiden Koffer, die durch einen breiten Lederspanngurt gegen jedes Verrutschen gesichert werden können. Sie sind in ihren Abmessungen genau dem zur Verfügung stehenden Raum angepaßt.

Mit wenigen Handgriffen kann die Fondsitzanlage in einen zusätzlichen Kofferraum verwandelt werden. Zwei große, auf Wunsch lieferbare Schrankkoffer, ja selbst sperrige Gepäckstücke, haben hier bequem Platz.

Zwei breite, harmonisch der Wagenform angepaßte Chromleisten am Heck nehmen die kombinierten Schluß- und Bremsleuchten, Blinklichter u. Rückfahrscheinwerfer auf.

Practical Elegance
The lengthened, elegantly curved rear encloses a spacious luggage compartment. Without spoiling the flowing exterior lines, room for two large special suitcases has been created here. The wide trunk lid can be raised effortlessly thanks to the built-in equalizing springs, and stays in its highest position with no trouble. At the same time, the luggage compartment light switches on automatically. The spare wheel is stored in a standing position at the right, easily accessible even with a full load. An additional spare wheel can be added optionally, which can be stored in a second well at the left—closed off with a cover as standard equipment. The two suitcases, which can be secured from any sliding by a wide leather belt—are part of the standard equipment. They are designed so that their dimensions exactly fit the available space.
With a few twists of the wrist, the rear seat can be turned into an additional luggage space. Two large self-locking suitcases, optionally available, have plenty of room here.

39

Practical Beauty

The sensible arrangement of all the instruments on the dashboard, the special conveniences for driver and passengers, and the beauty of the polished hardwood paneling give the 300 S its individual style here too. The carefree safety with which one can utilize the power reserves of the strong engine is a result of the operating technology that is aimed completely at thorough driving pleasure. The roomy, locking glove compartment has its own light. Its lid, when opened during a trip, can serve as a handy little table.

The wealth of equipment on the dashboard includes not only all the instruments and gauges for a trouble-free and safe journey, but also many special features that increase comfort.

In the large, glare-free, illuminated combined instrument, the speedometer with overall and daily odometers, oil-pressure and water temperature gauges, ammeter, fuel gauge, indicator lights and the switch for the adjustable instrument lighting are combined.

The parking lights can be switched off individually.

The octane compensator allows the exact setting of the ignition timing and assures the evenly high engine performance of the 300 S.

From the ashtray via the cigarette lighter to the illuminated glove compartment, from the two-speed windshield washer via the optional radio to the reading light, all the features of the 300 S are realized that satisfy even pampered tastes and emphasize the elite nature of this grand touring car.

As a particularly practical detail, a plug for a light or other electric device is included.
A knob on the lower left edge of the dashboard turns on the ventilating fan. The adjustment of the fresh air and heater duct is made by the lever in the middle of the dashboard. The roof light can also be turned on and off from the dashboard.

The main light switch can be set in one of four position according to the light and traffic conditions. Thus the interior and exterior lighting of the 300 S can be suited completely to the prevailing conditions.

A control knob is used to operate the three tone horn.

Zweckvolle Schönheit

Die sinnvolle Anordnung aller Instrumente auf der Armaturentafel, die besonderen Annehmlichkeiten für Fahrer und Mitreisende und die Schönheit der polierten Edelholzverkleidung geben auch hier dem 300 S seine individuelle Note. Die mühelose Sicherheit, mit der man die Kraftreserven des starken Motors ausnutzen kann, ist ein Ergebnis der ganz auf vollendeten Fahrgenuß abgestimmten Bedienungs-Technik.

Der geräumige, verschließbare Handschuhkasten besitzt eine eigene Beleuchtung. Sein Deckel kann aufgeklappt während der Fahrt als praktisches Tischchen dienen.

Die reichhaltige Ausstattung des Armaturenbretts umfaßt nicht nur alle Instrumente und Kontrollanzeigen für ein müheloses und sicheres Fahren, sondern auch viele Besonderheiten, die den Komfort erhöhen.

○ In dem großen, blendfrei beleuchteten Kombi-Instrument sind der Geschwindigkeitsmesser mit Gesamt- und Tageskilometerzähler, Öldruckmesser, Kühlwasser-Thermometer, Amperemeter, Kraftstoffvorratsanzeiger, Kontrolleuchten und der Schalter für die stufenlos regulierbare Instrumentenbeleuchtung zusammengefaßt.

○ Die Parkleuchten können getrennt abgeschaltet werden.

○ Der Oktanzahl-Kompensator erlaubt die genaue Einstellung des Zündzeitpunkts und sichert die gleichbleibend hohe Motorleistung des 300 S.

○ Vom Aschenbecher über den Zigarrenanzünder bis zum beleuchteten Handschuhkasten, vom Scheibenwischer mit zwei Geschwindigkeiten über das auf Sonderwunsch eingebaute Radiogerät bis zur Leselampe sind alle die Annehmlichkeiten im 300 S verwirklicht, die auch verwöhnten Ansprüchen genügen und die Sonderklasse dieses großen Tourenwagens unterstreichen.

○ Darunter ist als besonders praktisches Ausstattungsdetail ein Stecker für eine Handleuchte oder sonstige elektrische Geräte eingebaut.

○ Ein Zugknopf an der linken Unterkante des Armaturenbretts schaltet die Belüftungsgebläse ein. Die Abstimmung der Frischluft- und Wärmezufuhr erfolgt über die Hebel in der Mitte des Armaturenbretts.

○ Auch die Deckenbeleuchtung kann vom Armaturenbrett aus geschaltet werden.

○ Der Hauptlichtschalter wird den Licht- und Verkehrsverhältnissen entsprechend in eine von vier möglichen Stellungen gebracht. Dadurch kann die Innen- und Außenbeleuchtung des 300 S den jeweiligen Gegebenheiten genau angepaßt werden.

○ Über einen Zuggriff schaltet man das Dreiklanghorn.

The elegant dashboard was like that of the sedan, and in side view one can recognize the flowing lines of the powerful Cabriolet A, that embodied the restrained power of this high-performance car most expressively.

Die elegante Form vollendeter Technik

Die Eleganz und Schönheit des 300 S Cabriolets findet ihre Ergänzung in der mühelosen Handhabung dieses schnellen Fahrzeuges. Auch am Steuer kann man sich dem einzigartigen Erlebnis des „offenen" Fahrens im 300 S hingeben, weil man bei jeder Geschwindigkeit und in jeder Verkehrssituation stets dem Gefühl überlegener Sicherheit vertrauen kann.

The elegant form of perfected technology
The elegance and beauty of the 300 S Cabriolet are matched by the carefree operation of this fast car. At the steering wheel too, one can give oneself over to the unique experience of 'top-down' driving in the 300 S, since one can always depend on the feeling of complete safety in any driving situation.

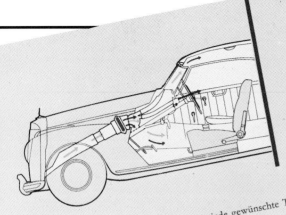

Sie fahren im Klima Ihrer Wahl

Left: The very effective heating and ventilating system was outstanding. In view of the relatively small window areas, the interior did not get warm quite as quickly as in present-day cars.

Von beiden Vordersitzen aus können Sie jede gewünschte Temperatur und Luftmenge individuell regulieren. Die Luft tritt unter Staudruck ein und wird über den Wärmetauscher in der jeweils gewählten Temperatur zum Wageninneren geleitet. Durch das vom Armaturenbrett aus einstellbare Verteilersystem kann die Warm- oder Frischluft getrennt zum Fußraum vor den Sitzen, zur Windschutzscheibe und zu den beiden Seitenscheiben geführt werden. Bei abgestelltem Motor sorgen zusätzlich zwei Gebläse für die unterbrochene Zuführung von Frischluft. Auch bei stärksten Temperaturunterschieden bleibt so eine einwandfreie Sicht durch die Scheiben erhalten. Damit dient das sorgfältig durchdachte Belüftungssystem nicht nur dem Wohlbefinden der Insassen, sondern auch ihrer Sicherheit.

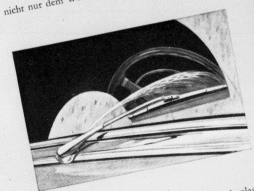

Auf Sonderwunsch wird eine Scheibenwaschanlage eingebaut. Während der Fahrt kann damit bei jedem Wetter die klare Sicht durch die Windschutzscheibe gesichert werden.

Ein Fingerdruck schaltet den serienmäßig eingebauten Blinkgeber für den Hauptscheinwerfer. Die Vorteile dieser „Lichthupe" zeigen sich besonders beim Überholen auf verkehrsreichen Straßen.

You drive in the climate of your choice.
From both front seats you can individually regulate any desired temperature and amount of air. The air enters under pressure and is conducted over a heat exchanger and into the interior of the car at the selected temperature. With the dividing system controlled from the dashboard, the warm or fresh air can be divided and directed to the foot space in front of the seats, the windshield and the two side windows. When the motor is turned off, two fans provide auxiliary power for the uninterrupted supply of fresh air. At even the greatest differences in temperature, a trouble-free view through the windows is thus maintained. The carefully planned ventilation system thus contributes not only to the comfort of the passengers, but to their safety as well.

A windshield washing system can be installed optionally. With it, clear sight through the windshield while driving can be assured.

A push of a finger switches on the standard blinker for the headlights. The advantages of this "light horn" are especially obvious while passing on roads with heavy traffic.

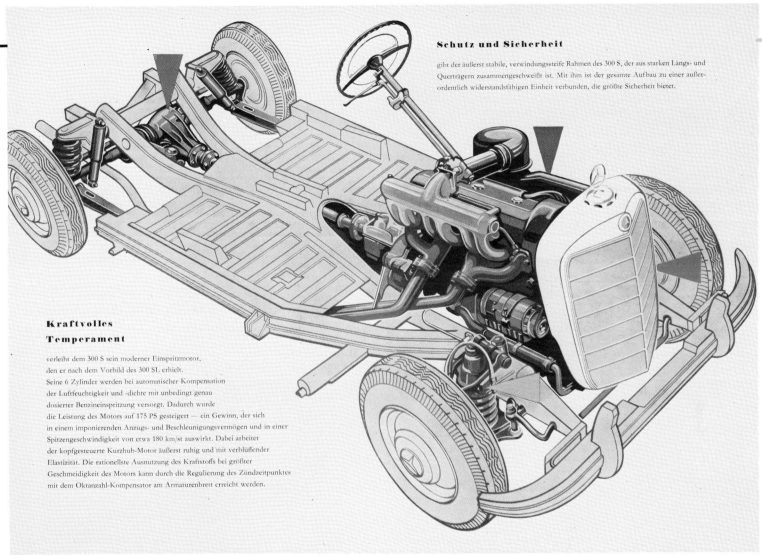

Schutz und Sicherheit

gibt der äußerst stabile, verwindungssteife Rahmen des 300 S, der aus starken Längs- und Querträgern zusammengeschweißt ist. Mit ihm ist der gesamte Aufbau zu einer außerordentlich widerstandsfähigen Einheit verbunden, die größte Sicherheit bietet.

Kraftvolles Temperament

verleiht dem 300 S sein moderner Einspritzmotor,
den er nach dem Vorbild des 300 SL erhielt.
Seine 6 Zylinder werden bei automatischer Kompensation
der Luftfeuchtigkeit und -dichte mit unbedingt genau
dosierter Benzineinspritzung versorgt. Dadurch wurde
die Leistung des Motors auf 175 PS gesteigert — ein Gewinn, der sich
in einem imponierenden Anzugs- und Beschleunigungsvermögen und in einer
Spitzengeschwindigkeit von etwa 180 km/st auswirkt. Dabei arbeitet
der kopfgesteuerte Kurzhub-Motor äußerst ruhig und mit verblüffender
Elastizität. Die rationellste Ausnutzung des Kraftstoffs bei größter
Geschmeidigkeit des Motors kann durch die Regulierung des Zündzeitpunktes
mit dem Oktanzahl-Kompensator am Armaturenbrett erreicht werden.

Protection and Safety

are provided by the especially stable, rigid chassis of the 300 S, which is welded together of strong longitudinal and transverse members. The entire body is attached to it to form an extraordinarily rigid unit that affords the greatest safety.

Powerful spirit

is given to the 300 S by its modern fuel-injection motor, like that of the 300 SL. Its six cylinders are supplied with the absolutely right fuel mixture thanks to automatic compensation for the dampness and thickness of the air. Thus the performance of the motor has been increased to 175 HP—a gain that shows in impressive passing and accelerating potential and a top speed of approximately 180 kph. And yet the short-stroke overhead-cam motor works especially quietly and with amazing elasticity. The most rational utilization of fuel and the greatest engine smoothness can be attained by regulating the ignition timing with the octane-count compensator on the dashboard.

A massive chassis according to old traditions also carried the body and the 175-HP motor of the additionally developed Type 300 Sc.

TECHNISCHE DATEN

Motor	Typ		M 199
	Arbeitsverfahren		Viertakt-Benzin-Einspritzung
	Motorleistung		175 PS**/5400 U/min (SAE 200 gr. HP/5500)
	Drehzahl bei 100 km/st		3440 U/min
	Höchstdrehzahl		6000 U/min
	Zylinderzahl		6
	Bohrung/Hub mm		85/88
	Gesamthubraum eff. cm³		2996
	Verdichtungsverhältnis		8,55 : 1
	Drehmoment max. mkg/n		26/4300 DIN (28,8/4500 SAE)
	Einspritzpumpe		Bosch PES 6 KL 70/320 RV 1235 (mit Regler PEZ 1562)
	Einspritzdüsen		Bosch DC 10 A 30 R 1
	Ölkühlung		Öl-Wasser-Wärmetauscher
	Kühlung		Wasserumlauf der Pumpe, Thermostat mit Kurzschlußleitung, Ventilator
	Ölfüllung		ca. 10 Ltr. Trockensumpf
Fahrgestell	Wechselgetriebe		Daimler-Benz 4-Gang vollzwangssynchronisiert, Lenkradschaltung
	Übersetzungsverhältnis		I. Gang 1 : 3,44 II. Gang 1 : 2,30 III. Gang 1 : 1,53 IV. Gang 1 : 1 R.-Gang 1 : 3,08
	Hinterachsübersetzung		1 : 4,11
	Lenkung		DB-Kugelumlauf mit autom. Nachstellung u. Lenkungsstoßdämpfer
	Höchstgeschwindigkeit im		I. Gang 54 km/st II. Gang 83 km/st III. Gang 127 km/st IV. Gang ca. 180 km/st
	Räder		Stahlblech-Scheibenräder
	Felgen-Größe		5 K × 15
	Reifengröße		6,50-15 extra spezial 6 Lagen
	Batteriekapazität		12 V, 70 Ah
	Hinterachse		DB-Eingelenk-Pendelachse m. tiefgelegtem Drehpunkt — Hypoidverzahnung
	Federn vorn		Schraubenfedern mit Zusatz-Gummifedern und zusätzl. Gummi-Horizontalfederung
	hinten		Schraubenfedern mit Zusatz-Schrauben- und Gummifedern
	Bremsanlage		Öldruckbremse mit ATE-Bremsgerät, Verbund-Bremstrommel, Leichtmetall-Grauguß mit Turbokühlung

Maße und Gewichte					
	größte Länge	mm	4700	Fahrgestell m. Aufbau trocken (ohne Reserverad und Werkzeug)	1660 kg
	größte Breite	mm	1916		
	größte Höhe unbelastet	mm	1510	Fahrzeuggewicht fahrfertig (Leergewicht nach DIN 70020)*	1780 kg
	Radstand	mm	2900		
	Spurweite vorn	mm	1480	Zulässiges Gesamtgewicht	2040 kg
	Spurweite hinten	mm	1525	* Leergewicht = fahrfertig mit Brennstoff,	
	Bodenfreiheit	mm	180	Reserverad und Werkzeug.	
	Wendekreis ⌀ ca.	m	12,3		
	Höchstgeschwindigkeit gestoppt ca.	km/st	180		

Kraftstoff
Kraftstoffnormverbrauch 12,5 Ltr.
(Ermittelt bei ²/₃ der Höchstgeschwindigkeit unter Zuschlag von 10%)
Tankinhalt 85 Ltr.
davon Reserve 6,5 Ltr.
Motoröl-Verbrauch 0,2 Ltr./100 km

Oktanzahl des Kraftstoffs Tankstellen-Super- bzw.
Benzin-Benzol-Kraftstoff mit mindestens 89 Oktan nach
Research-Methode (ROZ)

Steigfähigkeit

56 %

33 %

19 %

10,5 %

4.
3.
2.

** Die angegebene Leistung in PS ist nach Abzug aller Nebenleistungen an der Kupplung für den Antrieb des Wagens effektiv verfügbar. Bei der Leistungsangabe in gross-horsepowers sind die Leistungen der zum Motorbetrieb nicht erforderlichen Nebenaggregate unberücksichtigt.
Lt. VDA-Revers technische Angaben entsprechend DIN 70020 und 70030.

The new single-link swing axle allowed better road-handling as compared to the previous model. A 300 Sc cost 36,500 DM as of 1955.

Roadster

Favorit der Ans

With this 3-liter fuel injection motor, the 300 Sc attained a top speed of 180 kph.

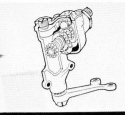

Der 300 S ist spielend leicht zu lenken. Jede Steuerungsbewegung wird über das bewährte Kugelumlaufsystem direkt auf die spurgenau laufenden Räder übertragen. So bleibt stets der notwendige Kontakt zur Fahrbahn erhalten, während umgekehrt Erschütterungen und Stöße elastisch abgefangen werden.

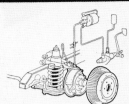

Der Schnelligkeit dieses sportlichen Fahrzeugs angepaßt sind die großdimensionierten Turbobremsen. Sie sprechen sofort an, packen weich aber fest zu und zeichnen sich durch hohe Standfestigkeit aus. Auch plötzliches starkes Bremsen erfordert nur einen geringen Kraftaufwand, da eine Unterdruck-Bremshilfe den erforderlichen Pedaldruck erheblich vermindert.

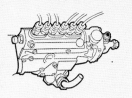

Die direkte Benzineinspritzung — einer der hervorstechenden motortechnischen Vorzüge des 300 S — arbeitet mit unbeirrbarer Präzision. Mit ihr wurde die Leistung des Motors auf 175 PS gesteigert und dabei der spezifische Verbrauch gleichzeitig gesenkt.

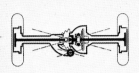

Die Eingelenk-Pendelachse, die zu einem Grundbegriff für die technische Fortschrittlichkeit aller Mercedes-Benz-Fahrzeuge geworden ist, liefert einen wesentlichen Beitrag zur idealen Straßenlage des 300 S. Sie besitzt nur einen tiefliegenden Drehpunkt. Dadurch wird die Schrägneigung der Räder (Sturz) erheblich vermindert und zugleich ihre Bodenhaftung verbessert.

The 300 S is playfully easy to steer. Every move of the steering wheel is transmitted directly to the accurately positioned wheels over the proved circulating-ball system. Thus the necessary contact with the road surface is always maintained, while in the other direction, disturbances and jolts are elastically absorbed.

The speed of this sporting vehicle is matched by the large-dimension turbo-cooled brakes. They act immediately, hold gently but firmly and prove to be highly effective. Even sudden hard braking requires only a small amount of power, since low-pressure power braking considerably decreases the necessary pedal pressure.

The direct fuel injection—one of the outstanding technological advantages of the 300 S—works with imperturbable precision. With it, the performance of the motor is raised to 175 HP and the specific fuel consumption is lowered correspondingly.

The single-joint swing axle, which has become a trademark of the technical progress of all Mercedes-Benz vehicles, makes a considerable contribution to the ideal road-handling of the 300 S. It has only one low pivot point. Thus the tendency of the wheels to tilt (toe-in) is considerably decreased and the road-handling simultaneously improved.

Favorite of the Demanding

With acceleration statistics almost equal to those of a competition sports car, and with its high speed, the 300 S Roadster offers the comfort of a large touring car. Sportiness and elegance unite with the proverbial "Mercedes-Benz safety" to make the 300 S the favorite of the international elite class.

Bei fast rennsportlichen Beschleunigungswerten und seiner hohen Geschwindigkeit bietet der 300 S Roadster den Komfort eines großen Tourenwagens. Sportlichkeit und Eleganz vereinigen sich mit der sprichwörtlichen "Mercedes-Benz-Sicherheit" und machen den 300 S zum Favoriten der internationalen Sonderklasse.

The heating system of the 300 S was developed and optimized by Behr of Stuttgart.

Right: A rare brochure for the large circle of Mercedes fans in the USA. As of that summer, a limousine lengthened by 20 cm, with electrically lowering glass panel behind the driver's seat, was optionally available.

Not only in the Federal Republic of Germany, where the Mercedes-Benz 300 with all its body types represented the pinnacle of car construction, but also in the USA, the land of opulent highway cruisers, did the German prestige car find a large number of admirers, and thus many cars made their way across the ocean, and some of them are now being re-imported by oldtimer collectors willing to pay the price. At that time, almost all the cars bought by Americans had automatic transmission.

ELEGANCE FOR THE CONNOISSEUR

Luxurious comfort, high performance and outstanding safety are the characteristic advantages which have put the 300 in the first international rank within a short time. Wherever it appears, the elegant lines of its body provoke spontaneous admiration. And now, in order to enable this splendid car to cruise smoothly along the ever more crowded roads of today, the Daimler-Benz AG has equipped the 300 with an automatic transmission.

The fact that this transmission effects all gearshifting operations automatically raises driving safety tremendously, particularly in the dense traffic of busy cities. Since you do not have to bother with a clutch pedal and gearshift lever anymore, you are free to concentrate on the oncoming traffic and are confident of mastering even the most awkward situations with your fast Mercedes-Benz 300 AUTO-MATIC. Even as you drive, you are able to relax and appreciate the thoughtfully-planned interior appointments and the feeling of buoyant gliding. Without abandoning the classic styling of the elegant body, Mercedes-Benz is proud to offer the 300 AUTOMATIC with all the advantages of modern automobile engineering. Now, more than ever before, owning this distinguished car means to be in the vanguard of technical progress.

Upon special request, the car can be supplied with a 4 in. longer body. In this way, there is 5½ in. more leg room at the rear. This design is particularly well adapted for the installation of a partition between the rear compartment and the driver's seat.

The 300 offered a welcome conservative
alternative in the land of the high-powered but
not always internally tasteful American cars.

Touring in spacious comfort

Comfortable, softly - sprung upholstered seats with ample leg room offer generous accommodation for 5–6 adults. The sumptuous materials, the polished wood mouldings, the large folding pockets and upholstered arm rests at the doors, the robe cord and luggage nets at the back of the front seats, and rails with clothes hooks above the side windows are some of the details which help to create an atmosphere of luxurious comfort. Upon special request, a de luxe radio, head rests at the front seats and other small things which make you feel at home can be installed.

The spacious luggage compartment in the elegant, well - proportioned rear holds even large trunks. Counterbalancing springs allow you to easily lift the locking lid which stays put in full - open position. A set of tailor - made suitcases will be supplied upon special request.

The technical equipment of the 300 AUTOMATIC has been further improved by the installation of the well-proved single-joint swing axle. Allied with the front wheel suspension and the effective brakes, it endows this fast car with an amazing roadholding and cornering ability. The flexible engine of the 300 AUTOMATIC develops 136 h.p. and is capable of reaching a top speed of very close to 100 miles per hour, whilst the standard fuel consumption remains at the low level of 22.6 m. per imp. or 18.8 m. per US gallon. The transmission's mode of operation has been exactly tuned to the performance of the engine. When the indicator on the steering column points to

"N", the engine is started by applying a slight pressure to the selector lever. To drive, the selector lever is merely set to "D". And now, regardless of whether you drive at a speed of 1 or 100 m.p.h., the transmission in each case automatically selects the most advantageous gear ratio. For steep gradients (driving over mountain passes) and abrupt descents, the indicator should be shifted to "L". If you wish to accelerate quickly, depress the accelerator pedal beyond the full throttle to kickdown position. This engages the next lower gear which can be operated up to its highest engine speed.

Not only is driving in the 300 AUTOMATIC safer and more comfortable, but the severe strains to which engine and transmission are frequently subjected in the course of daily operation are completely eliminated whilst service life is substantially prolonged.

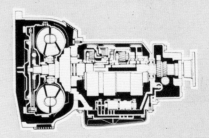

S P E C I F I C A T I O N S

Engine

No. of cylinders	6
Bore – Stroke	$3^{11}/_{32}$ ins. - $3^{13}/_{32}$ ins.
Piston displacement	182.8 cu. ins.
Engine output (SAE)*	136 b.h.p. at 4500 r.p.m.
Engine speed at 100 km/h (62 km/h)	3520 r.p.m.
Max. engine speed	6000 r.p.m.
Compression ratio	7.5 to 1
Carburettor	2 Solex compound carburettors
Capacity of cooling system, incl. heater	about 4.6 / 5.5 imp. / US gallons
Oil capacity of crankcase, max.	11.4 imp. pt. / 6.8 US qts.
min.	7 imp. pt. / 4.2 US qt.

Driving data

Max. speed of automatic transmission	about 97 m.p.h.
Climbing ability	max. 60 %

Chassis

Transmission	Detroit-Gear autom. transmission
Rear axle ratio	4.67 to 1
Tyre size	7.60 – 15 extra Special
Battery	12 V / 70 Ah
Rear axle	DB - single - joint - swing axle with low pivot point and hypoid gear

Fuel

Standard fuel consumption**	22.6 m. p. imp. or 18.8 m. p. US gallon
Tank capacity	15.8 / 19 imp. / US gallons
including reserve supply of	1.3 / 1.5 imp. / US gallons
Engine lube oil consumption	176 m. p. imp. pt. or 294 m. p. US qt.

Dimensions/Weights

Overall length	199 ins.
Overall width	$72^1/_2$ ins.
Overall height, unloaded	63 ins.
Wheelbase	120 ins.
Tread, front	$58^1/_4$ ins.
Tread, rear	60 ins.
Ground clearance (with 2 persons)	$8^1/_2$ ins.
Turning circle diameter	about 41 ft. 4 ins.
Curb weight of car	4210 lbs.
Max. total weight	5200 lbs.

* The output quoted in b.h.p. does not include the power for auxiliary units not required for engine operation.
** Determined at 2/3 of maximum speed less ten per cent.

Daimler-Benz, whose policy is one of continuous improvement, reserve the right to change designs, specifications, and equipment at any time without notice and without incurring obligation.

OUTSTANDING TECHNICAL FEATURES

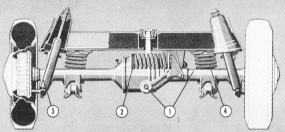

One of the most important contributing factors to Mercedes-Benz popularity and reputation among the world's finest cars, is the safety and roadability achieved through the use of the (1) Swing axle with its low pivot point which keeps both rear wheels in constant contact with the road. Standard equipment on all Mercedes-Benz cars.

(2) An extra compensating spring is furnished as standard equipment on all 190 series sedans, 220 series sedans, 220SE coupe and 300SL roadster-coupe. It provides an additional measure of safety for sharp cornering or high speed curves. (3) Telescopic, rubber mounted shock absorbers combined with (4) Heavy duty coil springs provide constant stability and riding comfort.

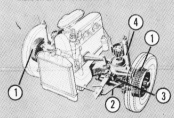

All Mercedes-Benz Models—except the 300 automatic 4-door hardtop, 300 4-door convertible and 300SL models—are equipped with a forward subframe assembly permitting removal of the complete front end chassis units for easy and more economical servicing.

(1) Finned brake drums dispel heat, reduce brakefade and increase lining life. (2) Torsion bar stabilizer (3) Coil spring suspension and (4) telescopic shocks provide excellent riding qualities and handling control.

Mercedes-Benz quietness and safety of operation are due, in part, to the rigid body construction. Great structural strength is achieved through the welding of the body shell to the sturdy, reinforced floor pan and frame, forming a quiet, distortion-free, twist-free unit. Engine noises are further isolated from the body by rubber mountings between the engine and subframe and between the sub-frame and main frame.*

*Except the 300 series cars which have their own exclusive frames.

MERCEDES-BENZ

300

CONVERTIBLE
AUTOMATIC

180 H. P. Manifold Fuel Injection Engine

Traditional Beauty . . . Modern Craftsmanship

The distinguished bearing of the Mercedes-Benz 300 Automatic 4-door convertible makes it perfect for formal occasions. At the same time, this car is equally at home cruising the highways with the proud owner's happy family. With top up, it is a luxurious sedan providing utmost privacy. With top down, it is a comfortable open touring car. Either way, it is an impressive-looking, high-performance vehicle with dignity and prestige in every line. Its design reflects the years of experience that Mercedes-Benz has had with this type of car. The manually adjustable top is easily opened or closed and its perfect fit guarantees a snug, weather-tight interior. Genuine leather upholstery is used throughout. Interior appointments and decor are in keeping with the Daimler-Benz fine car tradition.

For those interested in the Cabriolet D, there was a special American sales brochure with color photos, while drawings were still preferred in German catalogs.

Right: The American data sheet already describes the last 160 DIN-HP 300-D Cabriolet.

Chassis With Engine

The floor layout of the 300 Automatic Convertible is composed of two powerful longitudinal members welded to two lateral tubular bearers. This highly rigid structure is then firmly welded to the body.

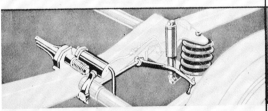

Auxiliary Suspension System

In order to maintain equally good springing action, even when the car is heavily laden, an auxiliary torsion bar suspension system has been produced for the 300 Automatic which can be actuated from the instrument panel by means of an electro-motor. If the rear seat is occupied by three persons, or the luggage compartment fully laden, this type of suspension completely compensates for these heavier demands.

Travel in Comfort and Safety

2-Way Adjustable Seat

The front seats may be adjusted lengthways by a movement of the hand while the back rests may be set at any desired angle. Comfortable head rests for the front seats may be supplied at extra cost. They are easy to install and remove.

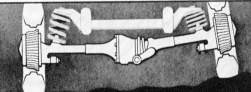

Swing Axle

The Mercedes-Benz single joint swing axle considerably influences the car's driving safety and curve stability. This time-proven engineering advance along with telescopic shock absorbers and independent wheel suspension of all four wheels provides an unusually well-balanced suspension permitting fast, safe driving even on rough roads.

SPECIFICATIONS
300 CONVERTIBLE AUTOMATIC

Engine

Type	6-Cyl. Overhead Cam and Valves
Bore and stroke	3.34 x 3.46 in.
Displacement	182.8 cu. in.
Horsepower	180 @ 5500 r.p.m.
Compression ratio	8.55 : 1
Oil Cooling	Oil-Water Heat Exchanger
Capacity of crankcase	4.25 qts.

Performance Data

Maximum speed in 4th gear 100 mph

Fuel

Fuel consumption	15 mpg
Fuel system	Intermittent manifold injection
Capacity of fuel tank	19 gals.
Including spare supply	1.6 gals.
Type of fuel	96 Octane min.

Chassis

Suspension, front	Independent suspension with coil springs, shock absorbers and torsion bar stabilizer
Suspension, rear	Independent suspension with coil springs, shock absorbers and auxiliary electric torsion bar suspension system
Rear Axle	Single joint, low pivot point swing axle.
Transmission	Automatic
Steering	Recirculating ball type, automatic adjustment
Brakes	Hydraulic, self energizing finned brake drums with power booster
Battery	12 volt — 70 amp. hrs.

Dimension and Weights

Overall length	204.3 in.
Overall width	73.25 in.
Overall height, unloaded	64 in.
Wheelbase	124 in.
Size of tires	7.60 x 15
Tread, front	58.2 in.
Tread, rear	60 in.
Ground clearance with 2 people, approx.	8.25 in.
Curb weight	4585 lbs.

Mercedes-Benz cars are manufactured by Daimler-Benz Aktiengesellschaft, Stuttgart-Untertuerkheim, and the company reserves the right to change designs, specifications, and equipment at any time, without notice and without incurring any obligation.

Mercedes-Benz vehicles are sold and serviced in the United States only through dealers authorized by

Mercedes-Benz Sales, Inc.
SOUTH BEND 27, INDIANA

Printed in U.S.A. Form No. P.S.P. – 113-9

300 SL *roadster*

Powerful sedan
and sports cars
from the house
of Mercedes-
Benz were and
still are the most
desirable cars in
the world for
many affluent
American
citizens.

300 *hardtop
automatic*

In a new garb of timeless elegance, the Mercedes-Benz 300 Automatic, with fuel injection, is introduced to you. Its modern exterior is matched by the design of its new interior decor. In addition, the 300 Automatic offers you heightened comfort the proved safety of its construction. The driving spirit of this large and strong car is characterized by the high performance of the new fuel-injection motor.

MERCEDES-BENZ

In einem neuen Gewand von zeitloser Eleganz stellt sich Ihnen der Mercedes-Benz 300 Automatic mit Einspritzmotor vor. Seinem modernen Äußeren entspricht auch die Gestaltung der neuen Innenausstattung. Darüber hinaus bietet Ihnen der 300 Automatic erhöhten Komfort und die bewährte Sicherheit seiner Konstruktion. Das Fahrtemperament dieses großen und starken Wagens wird durch die hohe Leistung des neuen Einspritzmotors charakterisiert.

300 Automatic

MIT EINSPRITZMOT

In August of 1957 the last version of the big Mercedes was officially introduced, with fully reworked and modernized bodywork and numerous technical improvements.

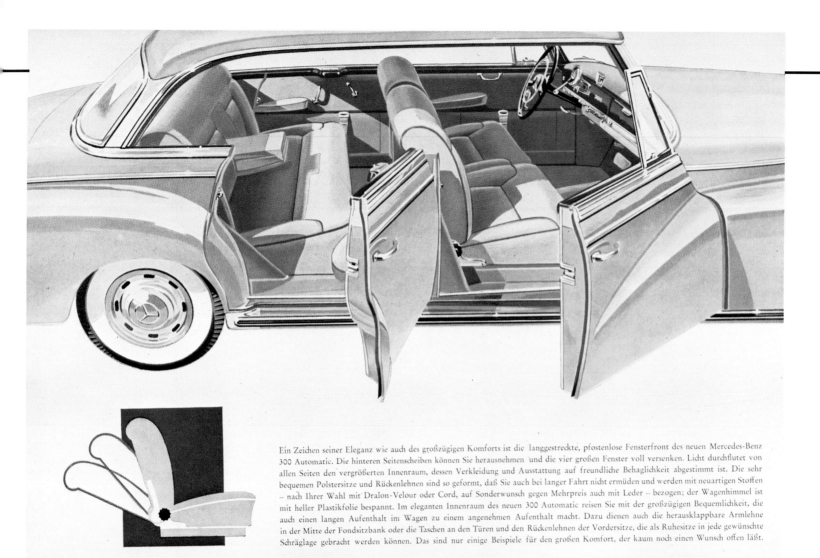

Ein Zeichen seiner Eleganz wie auch des großzügigen Komforts ist die langgestreckte, pfostenlose Fensterfront des neuen Mercedes-Benz 300 Automatic. Die hinteren Seitenscheiben können Sie herausnehmen und die vier großen Fenster voll versenken. Licht durchflutet von allen Seiten den vergrößerten Innenraum, dessen Verkleidung und Ausstattung auf freundliche Behaglichkeit abgestimmt ist. Die sehr bequemen Polstersitze und Rückenlehnen sind so geformt, daß Sie auch bei langer Fahrt nicht ermüden und werden mit neuartigen Stoffen – nach Ihrer Wahl mit Dralon-Velour oder Cord, auf Sonderwunsch gegen Mehrpreis auch mit Leder – bezogen; der Wagenhimmel ist mit heller Plastikfolie bespannt. Im eleganten Innenraum des neuen 300 Automatic reisen Sie mit der großzügigen Bequemlichkeit, die auch einen langen Aufenthalt im Wagen zu einem angenehmen Aufenthalt macht. Dazu dienen auch die herausklappbare Armlehne in der Mitte der Fondsitzbank oder die Taschen an den Türen und den Rückenlehnen der Vordersitze, die als Ruhesitze in jede gewünschte Schräglage gebracht werden können. Das sind nur einige Beispiele für den großen Komfort, der kaum noch einen Wunsch offen läßt.

One sign of its elegance as well as its great comfort is the long window surface, without posts, of the new Mercedes-Benz 300 Automatic. The rear side windows can be removed and the four large windows lower completely. Light flows from all sides into the enlarged interior, whose upholstering and furnishing are designed for friendly comfort. The very comfortable upholstered seats and seat backs are shaped so you won't get tired, even on a long trip, and are covered in modern fabrics—your choice of dralon velour or corduroy, or optionally with leather at extra charge—and the ceiling of the car is covered with bright plastic foil. In the elegant interior of the new 300 Automatic you travel in the greatest comfort that makes even a long time in the car a pleasant time. The folding armrest in the center of the rear seta bench, the pockets in the doors and the backs of the front seats, which can be adjusted to any desired position for resting, also contribute to your comfort. These are only a few examples of the great comfort that scarcely leaves anything to be wished for.

Es ist eine Frage Ihres eigenen Temperaments, ob Sie am neuen 300 Automatic mehr die Leichtigkeit des Fahrens oder seine Qualität und Zuverlässigkeit bewundern werden. Das automatische Getriebe schaltet für Sie, die Mercedes-Benz-Kugelumlauflenkung folgt Ihrer Hand leicht und genau, und die Servo-Bremse bedienen Sie so mühelos wie Sie fahren. Die Ausstattung des eleganten Armaturenbrettes aus poliertem Holz spiegelt den gehobenen Komfort dieses Wagens wider. Es enthält in klarer Anordnung alle zur Kontrolle und Bedienung Ihres 300 Automatic benötigten Einrichtungen. Starke Scheibenwischer mit zwei Geschwindigkeitseinstellungen, eine vorbildliche Heizung und Lüftung mit zwei zweistufigen Entfrostergebläsen, die Lichthupe, durch die auch das Horn betätigt werden kann, ein verschließbarer, beleuchteter Handschuhkasten, drei Ascher, die beiden gepolsterten Sonnenblenden und eine elektrische Zeituhr sind dazu noch einige Beispiele der großen Ausstattung, die das Reisen wirklich angenehm macht.

Das neugestaltete Heck des Mercedes-Benz 300 Automatic zeichnet sich durch drei besondere Merkmale aus: Der beleuchtete Kofferraum ist bedeutend vergrößert worden. Für Ihr großes und kleines Gepäck haben Sie damit den Raum, den Sie sich für weite Reisen wünschen. Die Heckleuchten sind größer und schöner geworden. Sie fassen die Blinkleuchten, Rück-, Brems- und Parklicht zusammen und enthalten serienmäßig einen Rückfahrscheinwerfer. Die neuen Stoßstangen laufen weit um das Wagenheck herum und sind von wuchtiger Stabilität. Die abgebildeten Weißwandreifen werden auf Sonderwunsch geliefert.

It is a question of your own personality as to whether you will give more admiration to the ease of driving the new 300 Automatic or its quality and reliability. The automatic transmission shifts for you, the Mercedes-Benz circulating-ball steering follows your hand lightly and accurately, and the power brakes serve you as easily as you drive. The equipment of the elegant dashboard of polished wood reflects the heightened comfort of this car. It contains, in clear order, all the facilities needed to control and operate your 300 Automatic. Strong windshield wipers with two speed settings, a superb heating and ventilating system with two two-speed defroster fans, the light flasher, by which the horn can also be used, a lighted, locking glove compartment, three ashtrays, two padded sun visors and an electric clock are several more examples of the fine furnishings that make travel really pleasant. The new rear design of the Mercedes-Benz 300 Automatic stands out in three special ways: The illuminated luggage space has been enlarged considerably. Thus you have the room that you need for your large and small luggage on long trips. The rear lights have become larger and look better. They include directional, brake, parking and taillights all together and include a standard back-up light. The new bumpers curve far around the rear of the car and are sturdy and stable. The illustrated whitewall tires are available optionally.

The major feature of the new body was the fully lowerable windows on the sides, which ventilated the interior splendidly in summer and made the car look even longer.

Above: A pleasant by-product of the now clearly more squared tail was a considerably enlarging of the luggage space, even though the standing spare wheel took up a lot of space.

Between 1957 and 1962, 3077 sedans with the 160 HP fuel injection motor were built.

The new three-liter engine with fuel injection develops 160 HP. This new design considerably increases the motor's torque. Thus the acceleration of the 300 Automatic has become even more powerful. To attain a completely even supply of fuel when starting, an auxiliary electric fuel pump was installed, which works automatically. The car owes its thoroughly dynamic spirit to this modern fuel-injection motor, and that spirit offers you a unique driving experience. And you can enjoy this experience in solid comfort, for the Mercedes-Benz Type 300 Automatic has been built carefully and tested thoroughly in every detail on the basis of absolute safety.

The Mercedes-Benz single-link swing axle, like the independent front suspension, provides for harmoniously balanced suspension. This design, proved a hundred thousand times, guarantees a safe and precise road-handling. Built into the very stable tube frame, the single-joint swing axle works together with a system of coil springs and telescopic shock absorbers.

To attain an equally good suspension effect under any load, the Mercedes-Benz Type 300 Automatic is equipped with an auxiliary suspension system. When the car is heavily loaded, you switch the electric motor of this auxiliary suspension on at the dashboard.

160 PS entwickelt die neue Dreiliter-Maschine mit inter-mittierender Saugrohreinspritzung. Diese neue Konstruktion erhöht wesentlich das Drehmoment des Motors. Dadurch ist die Beschleunigung des 300 Automatic noch kraft-voller geworden. Um eine völlig gleichmäßige Kraftstoff-förderung beim Start zu erreichen, wurde eine zusätzliche elektrische Kraftstoffpumpe eingebaut, die automatisch arbeitet. Diesem modernen Einspritzmotor verdankt der Wagen sein überaus dynamisches Temperament, das Ihnen ein einmaliges Fahrerlebnis vermittelt. Und Sie können dieses Erlebnis in aller Ruhe genießen, denn der Mercedes-Benz Typ 300 Automatic ist in allen seinen Teilen allein unter dem Gesichtspunkt absoluter Sicherheit für Sie kon-struiert, sorgfältig gebaut und gründlich erprobt worden.

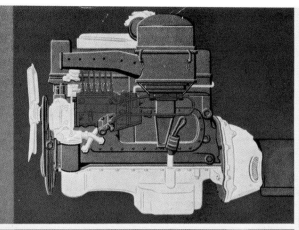

Die Mercedes-Benz-Eingelenkpendelachse trägt, wie die Einzelradaufhängung vorn, für die harmonisch ausgewo-gene Federung Sorge. Ihre hunderttausendfach bewährte Konstruktion garantiert eine sichere und spurgenaue Straßenlage. In den sehr stabilen Rohrrahmen eingebaut, wirkt die Eingelenkpendelachse zusammen mit einem System von Schraubenfedern und Teleskopstoßdämpfern.

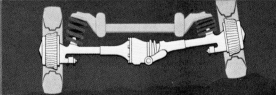

Um bei jeder Wagenbelastung eine gleich gute Federungs-wirkung zu erreichen, ist der Mercedes-Benz Typ 300 Automatic mit einer Zusatzfederung ausgerüstet. Bei hoher Belastung des Wagens schalten Sie vom Armaturenbrett aus diese Zusatzfederung über einen Elektromotor ein.

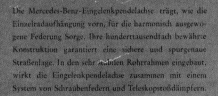

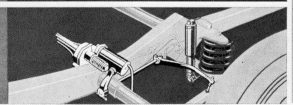

TECHNISCHE DATEN

Motor

Arbeitsverfahren	Viertakt-Benzin-Einspritzung
Zahl der Zylinder	6
Bohrung/Hub	85/88 mm
Gesamthubraum effektiv	2996 ccm
Motorleistung SAE	180 gr. HP/5500 U/min
DIN*	160 PS/5300 U/min
Drehzahl bei 100 km/std	3460 U/min (bei 1:4,67)
Höchstdrehzahl	6000 U/min
Verdichtung	8,55:1
Ölfüllung des Kurbelgehäuses max./min.	6,5/4,5 Ltr.

Fahrwerte

Höchstgeschwindigkeit b. autom. Getriebe	ca.165 km/std
Steigfähigkeit bei autom. Getriebe	max. 60 %

Fahrgestell

Wechselgetriebe***	Detroit-Gear-Getriebeautomat
Hinterachsübersetzung	1:4,67
Reifengröße	7,60–15 extra Spezial
Batterie	12 V/70 Ah
Hinterachse	DB-Eingelenk-Pendelachse m.tiefgel. Drehpunkt und Hypoidverzahnung
Bremsanlage	Öldruck-Vierradbremse mit verstärktem ATE-Bremsgerät T 50/12, Turbokühlung

Kraftstoff

Fahrverbrauch bei durchschnitt-lichen Überlandfahrten	11,5 bis 17 Ltr./100 km
Kraftstoffverbrauch nach DIN70030**	15,8 Ltr./100 km (gem.b.110 km/std)
Oktanzahl des Kraftstoffs	Tankstellen-Super- bzw. Benzin-Benzol-Kraftstoff mit mind. 86 Oktan nach Research-Methode (ROZ)
Tankinhalt	72 Ltr.
davon Reserve	6 Ltr.

Maße/Gewichte

Größte Länge	5190 mm
Größte Breite	1860 mm
Größte Höhe, unbelastet	1600 mm
Radstand	3150 mm
Bodenfreiheit (mit 2 Personen besetzt)	215 mm
Fahrzeuggewicht fahrfertig	2000 kg
Nutzlast	450 kg
Zulässiges Gesamtgewicht	2450 kg

Die angegebene Leistung in PS ist, da alle Neben-leistungen bereits abgezogen sind, an der Kupp-lung für den Antrieb des Wagens effektiv verfügbar.

** *Ermittelt bei ³/₄ der Höchstgeschwindigkeit, max. 110 km/std, zuzüglich 10 %.*

*** *Auf Wunsch auch mit Viergang-Schaltgetriebe lieferbar.*

Änderungen in Konstruktion u. Ausstattung vorbehalten

Ihr guter Stern auf allen Straßen

DAIMLER-BENZ AKTIENGESELLSCHAFT STUTTGART-UNTERTÜRKHEIM

Printed in Germany 374

The last chapter in the developmental history of the "Adenauer Limousine" was the Type 300 d. Its hardtop styling made it a lot more modern in terms of appearance, unlike its predecessors, which had come to look rather old-fashioned. These cars were now equipped almost exclusively with an automatic transmission, and a new era in interior design dawned with the use of collision-safe controls.

heute Spiegelbild des Fortschritts

Today a mirror of progress

Despite the more severe styling, still an impressive appearance: the 300 d from the front.

A glittering experience

Ein glanzvolles Erlebnis

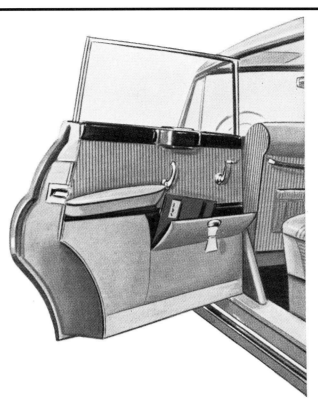

The standard 300 d had a longer wheelbase than previous models and offered its passengers a great deal of space. One could comfortably cross one's legs in the back seat, and no central window post disturbed the view to the sides.

Großer Raum mit großem Komfort

Überdurchschnittliches Niveau im Raumkomfort ist für einen Mercedes-Benz seit jeher selbstverständlich, doch was Ihnen der 300 Automatic bietet, geht weit darüber hinaus. Über zwei Quadratmeter Glasfläche umrahmen den um 14 cm verlängerten, lichtdurchfluteten Innenraum, der jede erdenkliche Bequemlichkeit für Sie bereithält: Sie können zu Hause nicht bequemer sitzen als in den weichen, nach medizinischen Erkenntnissen geformten Polstersitzen, die wie die Seitenverkleidungen mit werthaltigem Cord oder Dralon-Velours bezogen sind. In einer freundlichen Atmosphäre reisen Sie ermüdungsfrei über jede Entfernung. Vier elegant geformte Armlehnen an den Türen und eine breite, herausklappbare Armlehne zwischen den Fondsitzen unterstützen diese Behaglichkeit. In die holzverkleideten Fensterschlüssel sind Aschenbecher eingearbeitet. Zwei gepolsterte Sonnenblenden, die rechte mit Make-up-Spiegel, Haltegriffe im Fond, vier große Türtaschen und zwei weitere Taschen an den Rücklehnen der Vordersitze sind nur ein Teil der großen Ausstattung dieses auch von innen modernen und repräsentativen Wagens.

Die Vordersessel sind mit einem Handgriff in Längsrichtung zu verschieben, und die Rücklehnen lassen sich in jede gewünschte Schräglage stellen. Für die Vordersitze werden bequeme Kopfstützen* geliefert, die leicht angebracht und wieder abgenommen werden können.

In den 300 Automatic läßt sich zwischen Vordersitzen und Fondraum eine Trennwand* einbauen. Ihr über die ganze Raumbreite reichendes Fenster ist voll zu versenken. Netztaschen, Haltegriffe und Heizungsbedienung an ihrer Fondseite lassen keinen Komfort vermissen.

Um Ihren individuellen Wünschen entgegenzukommen, wird die gesamte Sitzausstattung mit wertvollen Lederbezügen* geliefert.

* auf Sonderwunsch

Whoever wanted to could have a lowering glass panel installed so as to be able to have privacy if desired. The equipment of the 300 scarcely left any wish unfulfilled, and its exclusive quality could even be heightened with leather upholstery.

Great space with great comfort

Above-average conditions of space a| comfort have always been taken || granted in a Mercedes-Benz, but wh the 300 Automatic offers you goes | beyond that. More than two cubic mete of glass surround the interior, whi has been lengthened by 14 cm a| flooded with light, and offers eve imaginable comfort for you: You cann| sit more comfortably at home than the soft upholstered seats, design| according to medical information, th| are covered, as are the side panels, wi| costly corduroy or dralon velour. In | friendly atmosphere, you travel a| distance without getting tired. Fo| elegantly formed armrests on the doc| and a wide folding armrest between t| rear seats emphasize this comfort. As| trays are built into the wood-cover| window frames. Two padded sun viso the right one with a make-up mirr| handholds in the back, four large | pockets and two more pockets on t| backs of the front seats are only a part the superb equipment of this car that modern and prestigious inside too.

The front seats can be adjusted lo| gitudinally with one move, and t| backs can be adjusted to any desir| angle. For the front seats, comfortab| headrests* which can be attached a| removed easily can be ordered.

In the 300 Automatic, a dividing pane can be installed between the front a| rear seats. This window, extending t| full width of the interior, can be ful| lowered. Net pockets, handhol| a| heater controls on the back of it assu| you that no comfort is missing.

To satisfy your individual wishes, a| the seats can be covered with cos| leather upholstery.*

* Optionally available at extra charge

60

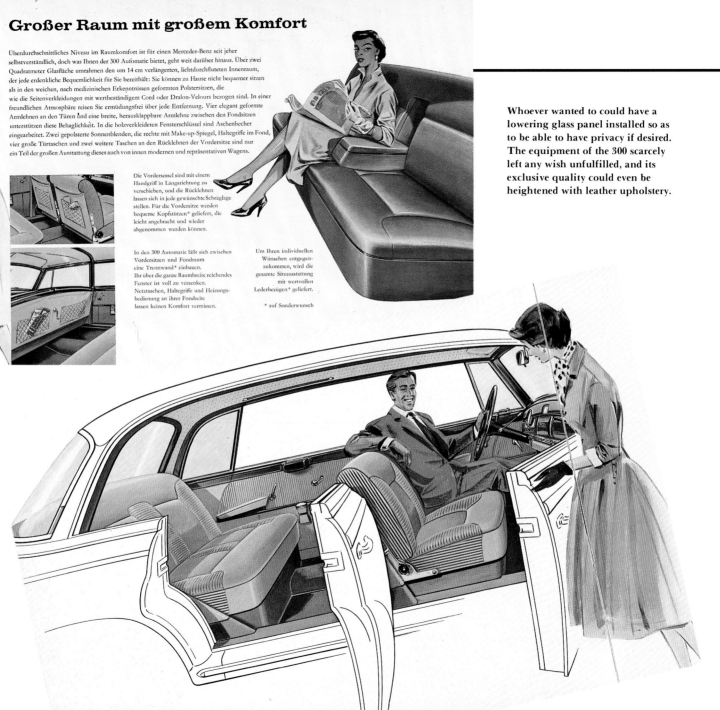

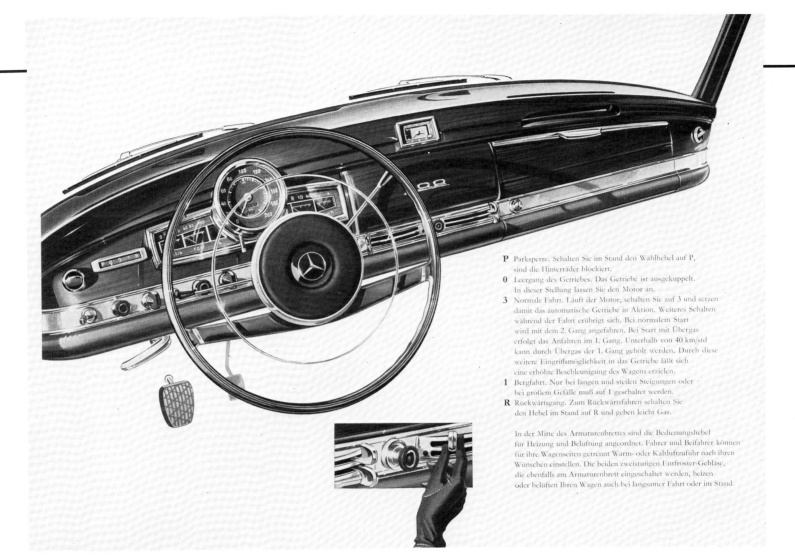

g lock. When you put the lever
...en the car is parked, the rear
...re locked.

...l. The gears are disengaged.
...t the motor in this position.

...l driving. When the motor is
..., you shift to 3 and thus put the
...ic transmission into action.
... shifting while driving is un-
...y. For a normal start, the car
...n second gear. When you start
...ll gas, first gear is engaged.
...0 kph, you can give full gas to
...first gear. This extra facility of
...smission lets you attain faster
...ion for passing.

...ar. You need use it only on long
...grades or steep downgrades.

...e. To back up, you move the
...om neutral to reverse and give
...tly.

...iddle of the dashboard are the
... for heating and ventilation.
...ver and passenger can set them
...ly for warm or cool air for their
... the car. The two two-stage
...r fans, with their switches also
...ashboard, heat or ventilate your
...n while driving slowly or
...g still.

P   Parksperre. Schalten Sie im Stand den Wählhebel auf P,
    sind die Hinterräder blockiert.
0   Leergang des Getriebes. Das Getriebe ist ausgekuppelt.
    In dieser Stellung lassen Sie den Motor an.
3   Normale Fahrt. Läuft der Motor, schalten Sie auf 3 und setzen
    damit das automatische Getriebe in Aktion. Weiteres Schalten
    während der Fahrt erübrigt sich. Bei normalem Start
    wird mit dem 2. Gang angefahren. Bei Start mit Übergas
    erfolgt das Anfahren im 1. Gang. Unterhalb von 40 km/std
    kann durch Übergas der 1. Gang geholt werden. Durch diese
    weitere Eingriffsmöglichkeit in das Getriebe läßt sich
    eine erhöhte Beschleunigung des Wagens erzielen.
1   Bergfahrt. Nur bei langen und steilen Steigungen oder
    bei großem Gefälle muß auf 1 geschaltet werden.
R   Rückwärtsgang. Zum Rückwärtsfahren schalten Sie
    den Hebel im Stand auf R und geben leicht Gas.

In der Mitte des Armaturenbrettes sind die Bedienungshebel
für Heizung und Belüftung angeordnet. Fahrer und Beifahrer können
für ihre Wagenseiten getrennt Warm- oder Kaltluftzufuhr nach ihren
Wünschen einstellen. Die beiden zweistufigen Entfroster-Gebläse,
die ebenfalls am Armaturenbrett eingeschaltet werden, heizen
oder belüften Ihren Wagen auch bei langsamer Fahrt oder im Stand.

The dashboard of the 300 d had
become safer but also more
restrained. A small indicator at the
left, near the combined instruments,
now showed the setting of the
automatic transmission.

61

The increase of 35 horsepower from the previous model was mainly attributed to the Bosch fuel injection pump and the increase of the compression ratio to a solid 8.55:1.

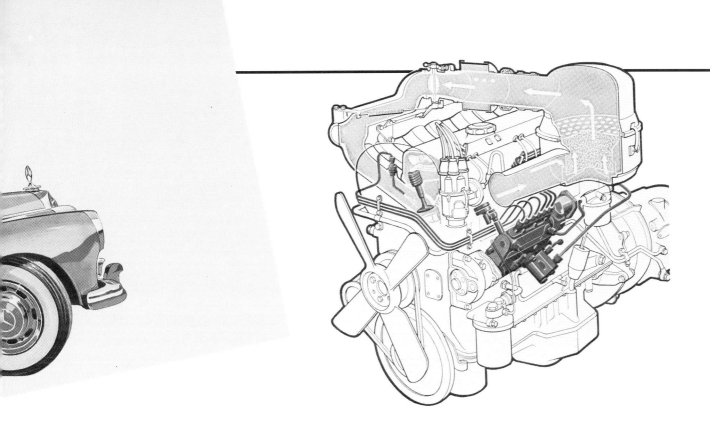

160 HP fuel injection motor—great power easily controlled

Such a big, strong, heavy car as the 300 Automatic can be driven with playful ease, which doubles the pleasure of every kilometer you drive. Declutching and shifting are gone from the 300 Automatic—the automatic transmission shifts for you. The steering follows your hand lightly and precisely (the car can be equipped optionally with power steering), and by using the gas and brake pedals, you have the 160 HP safely under control. The dashboard, a combination of practicality and elegance, has been refined in many ways for safety's sake. The steering wheel is now equipped with a protecting padded panel, and the control knobs are made of elastic material. A combined instrument informs you of speed, overall and daily mileage, oil pressure, water temperature, fuel level and battery charge. As examples of the great comfort, only the two-speed windshield wipers, three-tone horn, electric clock and flasher need be mentioned, the last of which—very subdued—is connected with the horn. With the foot control of the standard windshield washer you can also activate the wipers. In addition, there is a hand control for sustained wiper use. The locking lid of the glove compartment, which has an interior light, serves as a small table when opened.

160-PS-Einspritzmotor – große Kraft leicht beherrscht

Einen so großen, starken und schweren Wagen wie den 300 Automatic mit spielerischer Leichtigkeit in der Hand zu haben, verdoppelt die Freude an jedem Kilometer Fahrt. Kuppeln und schalten fallen beim 300 Automatic fort – das automatische Getriebe schaltet für Sie. Die Lenkung folgt leicht und präzise Ihrer Hand (auf Sonderwunsch wird der Wagen mit Servolenkung ausgerüstet), und mit Gas- und Bremspedal haben Sie die 160 PS sicher in Ihrer Gewalt. Das Armaturenbrett, eine Kombination von Zweckmäßigkeit und Eleganz, wurde in vielem, was der Sicherheit dient, noch verfeinert. Das Lenkrad wurde jetzt mit einer schützenden Polsterplatte versehen, und die Bedienungsknöpfe bestehen aus elastischem Material. Ein Kombi-Instrument unterrichtet Sie über Geschwindigkeit, Tages- und Gesamt-Kilometerstand, über Öldruck, Wassertemperatur, Tankfüllung und Batteriezustand. Als Beispiele für den großen Komfort seien nur zweistufige Scheibenwischer, Dreiklang-Horn, elektrische Zeituhr und die Lichthupe erwähnt, die – ganz heruntergedrückt – mit dem Tonsignal gekoppelt ist. Mit der Fußtaste der serienmäßigen Scheibenwaschanlage können auch die Wischer in Tätigkeit gesetzt werden. Außerdem ist ein Handschalter für Dauerlauf vorhanden. Der verschließbare Deckel des von innen beleuchteten Handschuhkastens dient aufgeklappt als Tischchen.

Auch die längste Fahrt ein sicherer Genuß

Der automatisch beleuchtete Kofferraum des 300 Automatic ist gegenüber seinem Vorgänger um 15% vergrößert worden. Damit bietet er jetzt mehr Raum, als selbst umfangreiches Gepäck füllen kann. Das Reserverad ist rechts stehend untergebracht und kann auch bei voll beladenem Kofferraum leicht herausgenommen werden. Übrigens erhalten Sie auf Sonderwunsch einen Satz Spezialkoffer.

Selbst für die weiteste Reise können Sie sich keinen idealeren Begleiter wünschen als den 300 Automatic. Seine Bequemlichkeit empfindet man gerade nach stundenlanger Fahrt als besonders angenehm, seine Zuverlässigkeit ist für Sie Gewißheit, und durch seine Erscheinung ist er überall in der Welt ein Botschafter kultivierten Geschmacks. Es spielt keine Rolle, wieviel Kilometer Sie diesem Wagen zumuten, und es ist ebensowenig von Bedeutung, wo Sie fahren. Durch seine Fahreigenschaften wird der 300 Automatic souverän mit allen Straßenverhältnissen fertig. Der Wagen kann auf Sonderwunsch auch mit Weißwandreifen sowie mit einem großen Stahl-Schiebedach geliefert werden, das Ihnen – wie beim Cabriolet – die Freude am „offenen" Fahren vermittelt. Ihrem Schutz dienen äußerst stabile Stoßstangen. Die Neugestaltung des Hecks ermöglichte eine beträchtliche Vergrößerung des Kofferraumes und den Einbau großer, formschöner Heckleuchten.

Even the longest trip is safe and pleasant

The automatically illuminated luggage space of the 300 Automatic has been enlarged by 15% from its predecessor. Thus it offers more room than even extensive luggage will fill. The spare wheel is housed standing up at the right and can be taken out easily, even when the luggage space is full. You can also obtain a set of special luggage optionally.

Even for the longest trip you cannot wish for a more ideal companion than the 300 Automatic. Its comfort feels particularly pleasant after hours of driving, its reliability frees you from care, and wherever in the world it appears, it is a sign of cultivated taste. It does not matter how many kilometers you put on this car, and it does not matter where you drive either. Thanks to its handling characteristics, the 300 Automatic can handle any road conditions easily. The car can also be equipped optionally with whitewall tires, as well as with a large steel roof hatch, that gives you the pleasure of "top-down" driving as in a convertible. Extremely stable bumpers serve to protect you. The new rear design made possible a considerable enlargement of the luggage space and the inclusion of large, beautifully formed taillights.

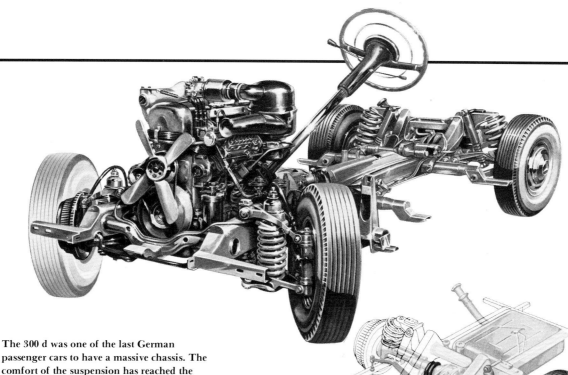

The 300 d was one of the last German passenger cars to have a massive chassis. The comfort of the suspension has reached the height of its development over the years; the 300 d was a very safe and pleasant vehicle.

The special functioning of the Mercedes-Benz single-joint swing axle contributes significantly to the good road-handling of the 300 Automatic. With only one low pivot point and long free-swinging half-shafts, the toe-in of the wheels is minimal. Thus the wheels adapt themselves smoothly to every road condition and driving situation with exceptional road-handling.

In order to maintain the same good suspension effect, even with a heavy load, an auxiliary suspension was created for the 300 Automatic. It is based on the principle of torsion-bar suspension and completely equalizes the car's heavy load. When the rear seat is occupied by three people or the luggage space is fully loaded, the auxiliary suspension can be switched on, its electric motor controlled from the dashboard.

When you drive your 300 Automatic, you will truly feel the safety with which it masters even the most difficult driving maneuvers. This safety is transmitted to you and is, in the end, the basis of unlimited confidence. Every technical detail of the 300 Automatic justifies this confidence. The road-handling begins with two strong longitudinal chassis members with tubular transverse members welded to them. This very stable construction is then firmly united with the bodywork. The motor is mounted on rubber cushions; thus the transmission of noise and vibration is hindered. A carefully balanced suspension system simultaneously gives the car outstanding road-handling and steadiness. The Mercedes-Benz circulating ball steering with automatic adjustment is additionally protected from road jolting by a steering damper.

Die besondere Funktionsweise der Mercedes-Benz-Eingelenkpendelachse trägt bedeutend zur guten Straßenlage des 300 Automatic bei. Durch nur einen tiefgelegten Drehpunkt und lange, freischwingende Halbachsen ist der Radsturz minimal. Dadurch passen sich die Räder bei ausgezeichneter Bodenhaftung jedem Straßenzustand und jeder Fahrsituation elastisch an.

Um auch bei hoher Belastung des Wagens die gleiche gute Federungswirkung zu erhalten, wurde für den 300 Automatic eine Zusatzfederung geschaffen. Sie beruht auf dem Prinzip der Torsionsstabfederung und gleicht die höhere Belastung des Wagens vollständig aus. Wenn die Fondsitzbank mit drei Personen besetzt oder der Kofferraum voll beladen ist, wird die Zusatzfederung vom Armaturenbrett aus über einen Elektromotor eingeschaltet.

Wenn Sie Ihren 300 Automatic fahren, werden Sie förmlich die Sicherheit spüren, mit der er selbst noch die schwierigsten Fahrmanöver meistert. Diese Sicherheit geht auf Sie über und wird schließlich die Grundlage uneingeschränkten Vertrauens. Jedes technische Detail des 300 Automatic rechtfertigt dieses Vertrauen. Die Bodenanlage setzt sich aus zwei starken Rahmen-Längsträgern mit eingeschweißten Rohr-Querträgern zusammen. Diese sehr stabile Konstruktion ist wiederum mit der Karosserie fest verbunden. Der Motor ist in Gummi-polstern gelagert; dadurch wird die Übertragung von Schwingungen und Geräuschen verhindert. Ein sorgfältig ausgewogenes Federungs-system gibt dem Wagen gleichzeitig eine überragende Straßenlage und Spur-sicherheit. Die Mercedes-Benz-Kugelumlauflenkung mit automatischer Nachstellung ist noch zusätzlich durch einen Lenkungsstoßdämpfer vor Fahrbahnstößen gesichert.

Technische Daten

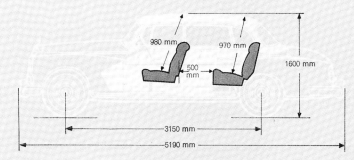

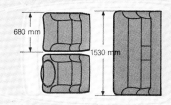

Kraftstoff

Fahrverbrauch bei durchschnittlichen Überlandfahrten .. 11,5 bis 17 Ltr./100 km
Kraftstoffverbrauch nach DIN 70030** .. 15,8 Ltr./100 km (gem. b. 110 km/std)
Oktanzahl des Kraftstoffs

Die Werkeinstellung des Motors erfolgt mit handelsüblichem Superkraftstoff
von OZ 93 bis 95 nach der Research-Methode (ROZ)

Tankinhalt (davon Reserve) .... 72 Ltr. (6 Ltr.)

*Die angegebene Leistung in PS ist, da alle Nebenleistungen bereits abgezogen sind, an der
Kupplung für den Antrieb des Wagens effektiv verfügbar. ** Ermittelt bei ¾ der Höchst-
geschwindigkeit, max. 110 km/std, zuzüglich 10%. *** Auf Wunsch auch mit Viergang-
Schaltgetriebe lieferbar. Änderungen in Konstruktion und Ausstattung vorbehalten*

Ihr guter Stern auf allen Straßen

Motor

Arbeitsverfahren .... Viertakt
Benzin-Einspritzung
Zahl der Zylinder 6
Bohrung/Hub .... 85/88 mm
Ges.-Hubraum effektiv .... 2996 ccm

Motorleistung
SAE .... 180 gr. HP/5500 U/min
DIN* .... 160 PS/5300 U/min
Drehzahl bei 100 km/std
3460 U/min (bei 1:4,67)
Höchstdrehzahl .... 6000 U/min
Verdichtung 8,55:1
Ölfüllung des Kurbelgehäuses
max./min .... 6,5/4,5 Ltr.

Fahrwerte

Höchstgeschwindigkeit .... ca. 165 km/std
Steigfähigkeit .... max. 60%

Fahrgestell

Wechselgetriebe*** .... Detroit-
Gear-Getriebeautomat
Hinterachsübersetzung 1:4,67
Reifengröße .... 7,60–15 extra Spezial
Batterie .... 12 V/70 Ah

Hinterachse
DB - Eingelenk - Pendelachse mit tiefge-
legtem Drehpunkt und Hypoidverzahnung

Bremsanlage
Öldruck -Vierradbremse mit verstärktem
ATE-Bremsgerät T 50/12, Turbokühlung

Maße und Gewichte

Größte Länge .... 5190 mm
Größte Breite .... 1860 mm
Größte Höhe, unbel. .... 1620 mm
Radstand .... 3150 mm
Bodenfreiheit .... 215 mm
Fahrzeuggewicht fahrfertig ..... 2000 kg
Nutzlast .... 450 kg
Zulässiges Gesamtgewicht ...... 2450 kg

Despite greatly
increased
performance,
the top speed
had scarcely
risen, with high
air resistance
being the
reason. When
the car was
packed to the
allowable gross
weight, it
weighed almost
two and a half
tons.

Technical Data

nsumption on usual overland driving: 11.5
ters/100 km
nsumption by DIN 70030**: 15.8 liters/100
easured at 110 kph)
count of the fuel: Factory adjustment of
tor is done with the usual super fuel of 93 to
ne, based on ROZ research.
capacity (including reserve): 72 liters (6

stated horsepower is, since all subsidiary
e already subtracted, that which is effectively
le at the clutch to propel the car.
termined at 3/4 of top speed, maximum 110
lus 10%.
lso optionally available with four-speed
al transmission.
ight to make changes in construction and
ment is reserved.

oning: Four-stroke gasoline fuel injection
er of cylinders: 6
stroke: 85/88 mm
acement: 2996 mm

rmance
180 gross HP at 5500 rpm
160 hp at 5300 rpm
ne speed at 100 kph: 3460 rpm (at 1:4.67)
engine speed: 6000 rpm
ression ratio: 8.55:1
kcase oil, max./min.: 6.5/4.5 liters

stics
speed: ca. 165 kph
bing ability: maximum 60%

ssis
smission:*** Detroit Gear automatic
axle ratio: 1:4.67
size: 7.60-15 extra Special
ry: 12 V/70 Ah
axle: DB single-joint swing axle with low
t point and hypoid gearing
e system: Hydraulic four-wheel brakes with
forced ATE T 50/12 brake apparatus and
o-cooling

ghts and Measures
rall length: 5190 mm
rall width: 1860 mm
rall height unladen: 1620 mm
eelbase: 3150 mm
und clearance: 215 mm
dy-to-drive weight: 2000 kg
wable load: 450 kg
wable gross weight: 2450 kg

Your good star on all roads.

P 1276 759 Printed in Germany

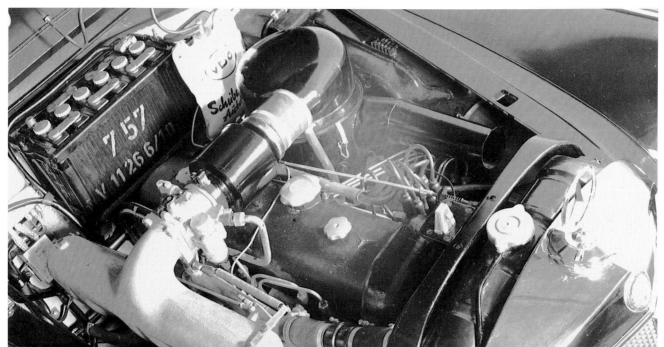

These rare factory photos also demonstrate the impressive details of the 300 d; even the small triangular windows behind the rear doors could be removed to evoke the atmosphere of a hardtop.

Below: An absolute rarity is this landaulet version of the 300 d Automatic, which was built for the Pope.

70

U. 9007

Hearses

The old established coachbuilding firm of Pollmann in Bremen specialized in the production of hearses and equipped a remarkably wide variety of vehicles, mostly German but also a few foreign marques, with special bodies. Mercedes-Benz vehicles, on account of their prestigious image, had always been the favorite basic models for such conversions, and remain so to this day. Whoever did not do without the comfort of a Mercedes while alive had a right to take his "last ride" in appropriate style.

Pollmann Coachbuilders
The Lines of Practicality

Pollmann Coachbuilders
Bremen, 9 Stresemann Street

oncept for thousands of bodywork
omers.
e nearly 200 specialist workers are
loyed to build special vehicles to
er. The following pictures show a
ll selection from the firm's old and
hearse models.
bear the same name:
mann Coachbuilders.

Pollmann Karosserie
Bremen · Stresemannstraße 9

für Tausende von Karosseriekunden ein Begriff.

Hier sind nahezu 200 Facharbeiter beschäftigt, um Sonderfahrzeuge nach Maß zu bauen.

Die folgenden Aufnahmen zeigen einen kleinen Ausschnitt aus dem alten und

neuen Bestattungswagenprogramm.

Alle tragen den gleichen Namen: Pollmann-Karosserie.

In dem neuen und umfangreichen DAIMLER-BENZ-Programm ist jede Fahrzeuggröße vorhanden. Die betont europäische Linienführung des Fabrikates wird auch im Aufbau fortgesetzt. Mit einer *Pollmann Karosserie* erhält der Käufer nicht nur einen eleganten Bestattungswagen, ein Transportmittel, sondern gleichzeitig 40 Jahre Erfahrung fortschrittlichen Fahrzeugbaues.

In the new and extensive Daimler-Benz program, every size of vehicle is available. The especially European styling of the vehicle is matched by that of the body. With a Pollmann body, the purchaser receives not only an elegant hearse, a means of transportation, but also forty years' experience in progressive vehicle building.

In a Pollmann catalog of 1966, four years after the "Adenauer" 300 went out of production, there is still a reference to a 300 hearse for particularly dignified clients.

Für die Winterausrüstung Ihres Mercedes-Benz

Personenwagen

	Für die Typen	Menge	Preise incl. Mont. u. Einbaumat. DM
Frostschutzmittel			
in Kannen		3 Liter	18.60
in Kannen		4 Liter	24.80
Mischungsverhältnis: für —20°C 33¹/₃ % Frostschutzmittelzusatz zum Kühlwasser			
Kühlerjalousien	170 V, Va, Vb, D, Da, Db, SV, SD, S, Sb, DS	1	64.—
dto.	180, 180 D	1	46.—
dto.	220	1	53.—
dto.	220a	1	46.—
dto.	300, 300 S	1	48.—
Fernthermometer	170 V, Va, Vb, D, Da, Db	1	39.50
Gebläse für Standbelüftung und Heizung	170 Va, Vb, Da, Db	1	59.—
dto.	170 SV, SD	1	69.—
dto.	170 S, Sb, DS, 220	1	74.—
dto.	180, 180 D, 220a	1	42.50
Nebellampen einschließlich autom. Relais-Schaltung			
Bosch, verchromt, ⌀ 105 mm......	180, 180 D	1	63.—
Bosch, verchromt, ⌀ 130 mm......	170 V, Va, Vb, D, Da, Db, SV, SD, S	1	68.50
Bosch, verchromt, ⌀ 130 mm......	180, 180 D	1	65.—
Bosch, verchromt, ⌀ 150 mm......	170 V, Va, Vb, D, Da, Db, S, SD, SV	1	74.50
Bosch, verchromt, ⌀ 130 mm......	170 Sb, DS, 220	1	62.50
Bosch, verchromt, ⌀ 150 mm......	170 Sb, DS, 220	1	68.50
Bosch, verchromt, ⌀ 105 mm......	180, 180 D	2	107.50
Bosch, verchromt, ⌀ 130 mm......	170 V, Va, Vb, D, Da, Db, SV, SD, S	2	113.50
Bosch, verchromt, ⌀ 130 mm......	180, 180 D	2	111.50
Bosch, verchromt, ⌀ 150 mm......	170 V, Va, Vb, D, Da, Db, SV, SD, S	2	125.—
Nebellampen			
Bosch, verchromt, ⌀ 130 mm......	170 Sb, DS	2	104.50
Bosch, verchromt, ⌀ 150 mm......	170 Sb, DS	2	116.50
Bosch, verchromt, ⌀ 130 mm......	220	2	108.50
Bosch, verchromt, ⌀ 150 mm......	220	2	120.50
Relais für automatische Nebellampenschaltung, **nachträglich** eingebaut		1	13.50

Sämtliche Preise verstehen sich einschließlich Montagekosten und Einbaumaterial.

4

Für die Winterausrüstung Ihres Mercedes-Benz

	Für die Typen	Menge	Preise incl. Mont. u. Einbaumat. DM
Rückfahrlampen			
Bosch, verchromt, rechteckig	170 V, Va, D, Da, Db, S	1	42.—
Bosch, verchromt, rechteckig	170 SV, SD	1	38.—
Bosch, verchromt, rechteckig	170 Sb, DS, 220	1	34.—
Handlampe mit 4,5 m Kabel, ohne Steckdose		1	14.05
Steckdose für Handlampe		1	6.25
Ski-Halter a. d. Dach anzubringen für 4 Paar Ski..................			Preis je nach Ausführung

Für die Pflege und Wartung Ihres Mercedes-Benz

Winteröle bekannter Schmierstoffmarken für Motor, Getriebe und Hinterachse

„Ferroxan" das Kühlerschutzmittel gegen Korrosion, Rost und Kesselstein. Löst Verschmutzungen des Kühlers, verhütet Rost und verhindert Schlammbildung.

		Menge	Preis
1 Rolle = 10 Tabletten ist ausreichend für eine Kühlerreinigung		1 Rolle	1.20
Kundendienst Durchsicht Ihres Wagens in regelmäßigen Abständen gemäß Scheckheft zu Festpreisen.			
Weiße Polierwatte		¹/₂ kg	4.45
„Mercedes-Neuglanz" für die Polierung von nitro-lackierten Wagen		¹/₂ kg	3.—
		1 kg	5.—
Mercedes-Benz Kunstharz Polish für die Polierung von kunstharz-lackierten Wagen		1 kg	9.80
Mercedes-Benz „Kristall" für die Nachbehandlung nach dem Polieren zur Konservierung der Nitro-Lackierung		¹/₄ kg	5.40
		¹/₂ kg	8.55
Mercedes-Benz „Brillant" für die Chrompflege		¹/₂ kg	3.60
Mercedes-Benz „Carneol" für die Lederpflege		¹/₂ kg	3.60
„Frillo"-Fleckenwasser zur Reinigung der Polsterung, Entfernung von Teerflecken und Rückständen an den Kotflügeln		1 Flasche	1.80

Sämtliche Preise verstehen sich einschließlich Montagekosten und Einbaumaterial.

5

73

Für Ihre Bequemlichkeit

	Für die Typen	Menge	Preise incl. Mont. u. Einbaumat. DM
Ruhesitze — Schlafsitze			
Verstellbare Rückenlehne der Vordersitze — Stoffbezug Innenlenker	170 V, Va, Vb, D, Da, Db, SV, SD, S, Sb, DS, 220, 180, 180 D, 220a	1 Sitz	110.—
Mehrpreis für Mitlieferung einer Kopfstütze einschl. 2 Schonbezügen und einer Schutzhülle — Stoffbezug Innenlenker	wie oben	1	140.—
Polsterschonbezüge			
Velveton in verschiedenen Farben, mit weißer Biese eingefaßt	170 S, Sb, DS, 220	Garnitur	191.50
dto.	180, 180 D	Garnitur	131.—
dto.	220a	Garnitur	215.—
dto. ohne Seitenteile	170 SV, SD	Garnitur	131.—
Schottenmuster	170 S, Sb, DS, 220	Garnitur	196.50
Schottenmuster	180, 180 D	Garnitur	136.—
Schottenmuster	220a	Garnitur	215.—
Schottenmuster, o. Seitenteile	170 SV, SD	Garnitur	136.—
Fußmatten			
Kokosmatten, 4-teilig	170 V, Va, Vb, D, Da, Db	1 Satz	20.50
Kokosmatten, 4-teilig	170 SV, SD, S, Sb, DS, 220	1 Satz	27.30
Kokosmatten, 4-teilig	180, 180 D	1 Satz	43.85
Kokosmatten, 4-teilig	220a	1 Satz	46.30
Kokosmatten, 3-teilig	300	1 Satz	59.80
Kokosmatten, 4-teilig	300	1 Satz	40.50

Sämtliche Preise verstehen sich einschließlich Montagekosten und Einbaumaterial.

Für Ihre Bequemlichkeit

	Für die Typen	Menge	Preise incl. Mont. u. Einbaumat. DM
Auto-Radio			
Fabrikat Becker „Solitude" 6 und 12 Volt	170 SV, SD, S, Sb, DS, 220	1	590.—
Fabrikat Becker „Monaco" m. Drucktasten, 6 und 12 Volt	170 SV, SD, S, Sb, DS, 220	1	675.—
Fabrikat Becker „Mexiko" vollautomatisch, 6 Volt	180	1	680.—
Fabrikat Becker „Mexiko" vollautomatisch, 12 Volt	180 D	1	645.—
Fabrikat Becker „Mexiko" vollautomatisch, 12 Volt	220a	1	695.—
Fabrikat Becker „Nürburg" mit Drucktasten	300, 300 S	1	850.—
Fabrikat „Telefunken" mit Drucktasten, 6 und 12 Volt	170 SV, SD, S, Sb, DS, 220	1	590.—
Fabrikat „Telefunken" mit Drucktasten, 12 Volt	180 D	1	395.—
Fabrikat „Telefunken" mit Drucktasten, 6 und 12 Volt	180, 220a	1	415.—
Fabrikat „Telefunken" mit Drucktasten	300, 300 S	1	670.—
Zugfreie Entlüftung			
an beiden vorderen Seitenfenstern	170 SV, SD, S, Sb, DS, 220	2	95.—
Innenkoffer			
3-teilig	170 SV, SD, S, Sb, DS, 220	1 Satz	275.—
4-teilig	180, 180 D, 220a	1 Satz	325.—
2-teilig, Ausführung I, bestehend aus: 1 Damenschrankkoffer mit Wäscheeinsatz 1 Herrenschrankkoffer mit Wäscheeinsatz	300	1 Satz	380.—
4-teilig, Ausführung II, bestehend aus: 1 Damenschrankkoffer mit Wäscheeinsatz 1 Herrenschrankkoffer mit Wäscheeinsatz 2 Hutkoffer	300	1 Satz	560.—
Kofferboden	170 SV, SD	1 Satz	27.50
Kofferraum-Beleuchtung	170 Va, Vb, Da, Db, SV, SD, S, Sb, DS	1	22.—
Kleiderhaken, verchromt		1	5.—

Sämtliche Preise verstehen sich einschließlich Montagekosten und Einbaumaterial.

The most popular special accessories for the already almost completely equipped 300 models were various push-button radios by Becker or Telefunken, at that time terribly expensive but very impressive, and luxurious custom-made sets of luggage.

Praktisches Zubehör

	Für die Typen	Menge	Preise incl. Mont. u. Einbaumat. DM
Rückwandfenster-Jalousie	180, 180 D, 220a	1	70.—
Tankverschluß, verschließbar		1	10.—
Rückstrahler		1	1.30
Feuerlöscher		1	32.50
Feuerlöscher, verchromt		1	37.—
Laufradringe, verchromt	170 V, Va, Vb, D, Da, Db SV, SD, DS	5	70.50
dto.	170 S, Sb, 180, 180 D, 220	5	60.50
Rückblickspiegel a. d. Tür		1	13.75
Rückblickspiegel (abblendbar, Kippspiegel)		1	20.50
Aschenbecher, im Fond Metall verchromt	170 V, Va, Vb, D, Da, Db	1	7.—
dto. — Glas	170 V, Va, Vb, D, Da, Db	1	4.90
dto. — Bakelit mit Chrom		1	8.—

Mehrklang-Signale

	Für die Typen	Menge	Preise incl. Mont. u. Einbaumat. DM
Hella-Schneckenhorn	170 SV, SD, S, Sb, DS, 220	1	98.50
dto.	180, 180 D	1	108.—
Bosch-Dreiklanghorn, 2 Zusatzhörner	170 V, Va, Vb, D, Da, Db SV, SD, S, Sb, DS	2	79.—
dto.	180, 180 D	2	84.—
Bosch-Starktonhorn	170 V, Va, Vb, D, Da, Db SV, SD, S, Sb, DS	1	43.—
Bosch-Doppelton, Fanfare	180	1	118.—
dto.	180 D	1	129.—
dto. in Silberlack	220a	1	140.—
Bosch-Zweiklanghorn, 1 Zusatzhorn	170 V, Va, Vb, D, Da, Db SV, SD, S, Sb, DS	1	28.—

Sämtliche Preise verstehen sich einschließlich Montagekosten und Einbaumaterial.

8

Praktisches Zubehör

	Für die Typen	Menge	Preise incl. Mont. u. Einbaumat. DM
D-Buchstabe, verchromt unbeleuchtet		1	8.90
D-Schild mit Chromrand unbeleuchtet	170 V, Va, Vb, D, Da, Db, SV, SD	1	8.40
D-Schild mit Flutlicht-Beleuchtung, SWF, rechts auf der hinteren Stoßstange	170 V, Va, Vb, D, Da, Db, SV, SD	1	31.30
D-Schild mit Chromrand beleuchtbar, ohne Stoßstangenhorn	170 Sb, DS, 220	1	6.—
D-Schild mit Chromrand beleuchtbar, mit Stoßstangenhorn	170 S, Sb, DS	1	20.70
D-Schild mit Chromrand beleuchtbar durch Nummernbeleuchtung ..	180, 180 D, 220a	1	6.—
Reserverad-Halter, schwenkbar, lackiert, mit Schloß und Zierdeckel, ohne Reifen und Felge	170 SV, SD, S, Sb, DS, 220	1	130.—
Reserverad-Abdeckblech mit Chromring, passend zur Wagenfarbe lackiert	170 V, Va, Vb, D, Da, Db	1	50.—
Sicherungsschloß für Reserverad	170 V, Va, Vb, D, Da, Db	1	5.80
Sonnenblende		1	15.40
Kanister für Brennstoffreserve Allboy m. Einfüllstutzen, 5 Ltr. ...		1	22.15
Allboy m. Einfüllstutzen, 10 Ltr.		1	24.15
10-Liter-Kanister		1	18.50
Einfüllstutzen dazu		1	6.—

Sämtliche Preise verstehen sich einschließlich Montagekosten und Einbaumaterial.

9

75

Praktisches Zubehör

	Für die Typen	Menge	Preise incl. Mont. u. Einbaumat. DM
Nummernschild-Verstärkung			
mit Chromrand	170 SV, SD, S, Sb, DS, 220	2	8.—
dto. nur vorne	180, 180 D	1	4.—
Weißes Lenkrad und weißer Schalthebelknopf, unter Verwendung des vorhandenen Signalringes	170 V, Va, Vb, D, Da, Db, SV, SD, S, Sb, DS, 220	1	38.—
dto.	180, 180 D, 220a	1	48.30
Weißes Lenkrad mit verchromtem Signalring und weißem Schalthebelknopf	170 V, Va, Vb, D, Da, Db, S	1	53.—
Blumenvase		1	6.—
Auspuffblende, verchromt		1	6.—
Steinschlag-Schutzgummi für Hinterkotflügel	170 V, Va, Vb, D, Da, Db, SV, SD, S, Sb, DS, 220	2	20.20
Reifendruckprüfer		1	6.50
2. Reserverad m. Halterung dazu ..	180, 180 D	1	125.—
dto.	220a	1	143.—
1 kleiner Satz Bordwerkzeuge			
ohne Wagenheber	170 V, Va, Vb	1 Satz	19.10
dto.	170 D, Da, Db	1 Satz	26.95
dto.	170 SV, SD, S, Sb, DS	1 Satz	25.60
dto.	220	1 Satz	33.45
dto.	180	1 Satz	25.75
dto.	180 D	1 Satz	19.70
Kasten mit 1 Satz Autolampen und Sicherungen		1	15.75
Verbandkasten für „Erste Hilfe" (ohne Montage)		je nach Größe	

Sämtliche Preise verstehen sich einschließlich Montagekosten und Einbaumaterial.

10

Für die Winterausrüstung Ihres Mercedes-Benz

	Für die Typen	Menge	Preise incl. Mont. u. Einbaumat. DM
Frostschutzmittel			
in Kannen		3 Liter	18.60
in Kannen		4 Liter	24.80
Mischungsverhältnis: für —20°C 33 1/3 % Frostschutzmittelzusatz zum Kühlwasser			
Kühlerjalousie	L u. O 3500, L 4500	1	76.50
Nebellampen einschließlich autom. Relais-Schaltung			
Bosch, verchromt, ⌀ 130 mm	L 3500, L 4500 L 5500 bzw. L 325-6 to-Kl. L 6600 bzw. L 315-7 to-Kl.	1	71.50
Bosch, verchromt, ⌀ 150 mm	wie oben	1	77.20
Bosch, verchromt, ⌀ 130 mm	wie oben	2	117.50
Bosch, verchromt, ⌀ 150 mm	wie oben	2	129.20

Sonderausrüstung

	Für die Typen	Menge	Preise incl. Mont. u. Einbaumat. DM
Rückfahrlampen			
Bosch, verchromt, ⌀ 130 mm	L 3500, L 4500 L 5500 bzw. L 325-6 to-Kl. L 6600 bzw. L 315-7 to-Kl.	1	61.50
Notek, verchromt, ⌀ 105 mm mit Steinschlagschutz	wie oben	1	64.50
Dreieck-Rückstrahler	LKW u. LKW-Anhänger	2	28.—
Großes Schluß-Stopplicht auf der Seite der Nummerntafel		1	22.—
dto. gegenüber der Nummerntafel..		1	29.—

Sämtliche Preise verstehen sich einschließlich Montagekosten und Einbaumaterial.

11

Sonderausrüstung

	Für die Typen	Menge	Preise incl. Mont. u. Einbaumat. DM
Sonnenblende		1	22.50
Begrenzungsstangen	L u. O 3500	2	24.50
Zweiter Rückblickspiegel			
rechts am Fahrerhaus		1	7.90
Gummi-Spritzlappen			
für Hinterkotflügel	L 3500, L 4500	2	20.—
dto.	L 5500 bzw. L 325-6 to-Kl. L 6600 bzw. L 315-7 to-Kl.	2	25.—
Zeitweg-Schreiber (Tachograph)			
nachträglich eingebaut	L u. O 3500	1	257.—
dto.	L 5000, O 6600 L 5500 bzw. L 325-6 to-Kl. L 6600 bzw. L 315-7 to-Kl.	1	282.—
Zeitweg-Schreiber Tachograph für			
7 Tage, nachträglich eingebaut	L u. O 3500	1	279.—
dto.	L 5000 L 5500 bzw. L 325-6 to-Kl. L 6600 bzw. L 315-7 to-Kl.	1	297.—
Druckluftbremse			
nachträglich eingebaut	L 3500	1	975.—

Sämtliche Preise verstehen sich einschließlich Montagekosten und Einbaumaterial.

Sonderausrüstung

	Für die Typen	Menge	Preise incl. Mont. u. Einbaumat. DM
Motorbremse			
nachträglich eingebaut	L 3500, L 4500	1	315.—
dto.	O 3500	1	304.—
dto. — Motor OM 67/4	L 5000	1	438.—
dto. — Motor OM 67/8	L 5000 L 5500 bzw. L 325-6 to-Kl.	1	395.50
dto.	O 5000	1	463.—
dto.	L 6600 bzw. L 315-7 to-Kl.	1	378.—
dto.	O 6600	1	378.—
dto.	O 6600 H	1	459.50

> **Preisänderungen vorbehalten!**
> Sämtliche Preise verstehen sich einschließlich Montagekosten. Die Preise gelten für die normale Anbringungsart und bei Personenwagen für den Innenlenker.

For the other, "smaller" Mercedes models there was a much greater variety of possible accessories to choose from; who ever wanted to equip his 300 with coconut mats?

Brilliant Technology

The Mercedes-Benz Type 300, in all its luxurious and sporting varieties, offered not only a high degree of quality handcrafting, but also, despite its conservative appearance, had a wealth of highly developed and effective technical features to offer, which despite all their complexity guaranteed a great deal of reliability and did their part to maintain the extraordinarily high reputation of the tradition-rich Swabian automotive firm.

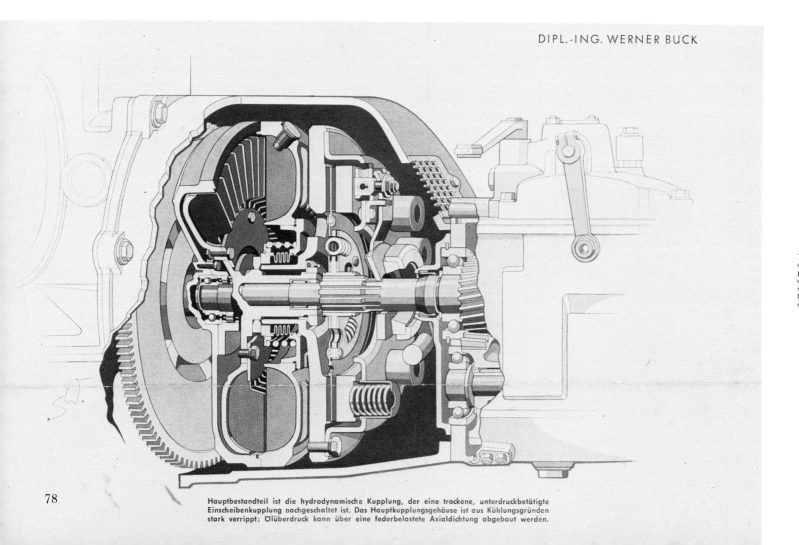

DIPL.-ING. WERNER BUCK

Engineer Werner Buck
The main component is the hydr[o]dynamic clutch, to which a dry sing[le] plate clutch activated by low pressure [is] connected. The main clutch housing [is] strongly ribbed for the sake of cool[ing;] high oil pressure can be released via spring-operated axial reinforcement.

Hauptbestandteil ist die hydrodynamische Kupplung, der eine trockene, unterdruckbetätigte Einscheibenkupplung nachgeschaltet ist. Das Hauptkupplungsgehäuse ist aus Kühlungsgründen stark verrippt; Ölüberdruck kann über eine federbelastete Axialdichtung abgebaut werden.

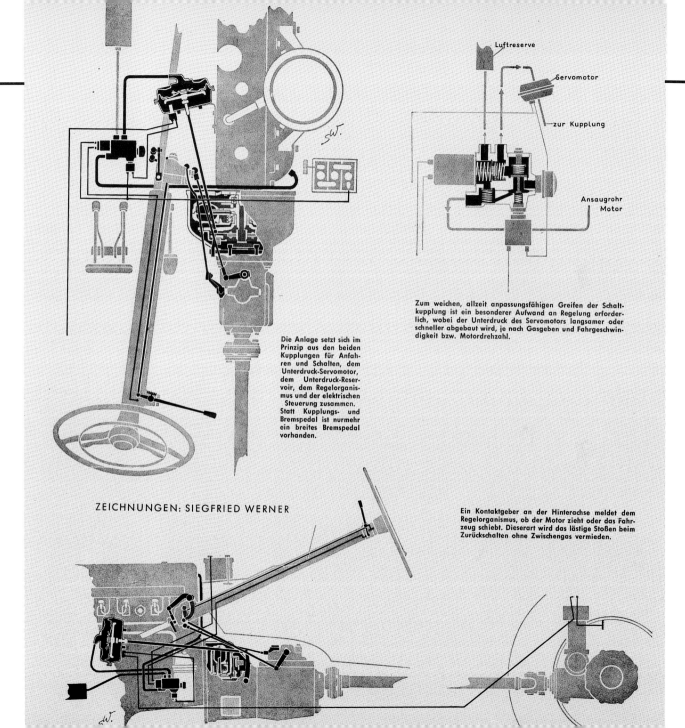

The system is based in principle on the two clutches for starting and shifting, the low-pressure servo motor, the low-pressure reservoir, the regulator and the electric controls. Instead of clutch and brake pedals, there is now only a wide brake pedal.

Air reserve
Servo motor
To the clutch
Intake pipe
Motor

For soft, always appropriate gripping of the shifting clutch, a particular amount of regulation is required, whereby the low pressure of the servo motor is released slowly or quickly according to how much gas is given and how fast the car or motor is running.

A contact point on the rear axle reports to the regulator as to whether the motor is pulling or the vehicle pushing. In this way the burdening of the motor while downshifting without double-clutching is avoided.

Drawings: Siegfried Werner

Luftreserve
Servomotor
zur Kupplung
Ansaugrohr Motor

Zum weichen, allzeit anpassungsfähigen Greifen der Schaltkupplung ist ein besonderer Aufwand an Regelung erforderlich, wobei der Unterdruck des Servomotors langsamer oder schneller abgebaut wird, je nach Gasgeben und Fahrgeschwindigkeit bzw. Motordrehzahl.

Die Anlage setzt sich im Prinzip aus den beiden Kupplungen für Anfahren und Schalten, dem Unterdruck-Servomotor, dem Unterdruck-Reservoir, dem Regelorganismus und der elektrischen Steuerung zusammen. Statt Kupplungs- und Bremspedal ist nurmehr ein breites Bremspedal vorhanden.

ZEICHNUNGEN: SIEGFRIED WERNER

Ein Kontaktgeber an der Hinterachse meldet dem Regelorganismus, ob der Motor zieht oder das Fahrzeug schiebt. Dieserart wird das lästige Stoßen beim Zurückschalten ohne Zwischengas vermieden.

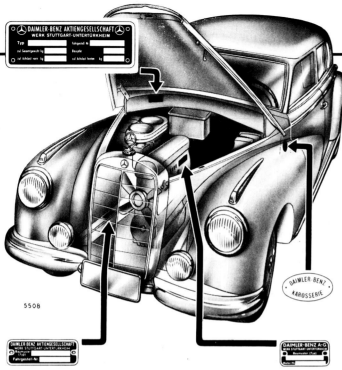

5508

This drawing in the service manual indicated the points at which body and motor labels were to be found, important for definite identification of old cars.

Not so very confusing, even for the layman: the shifting chart for a 300 with carburetor motor.

It is surprising how much work had to be done during servicing not so long ago, as shown here by the lubricating chart for the 300.

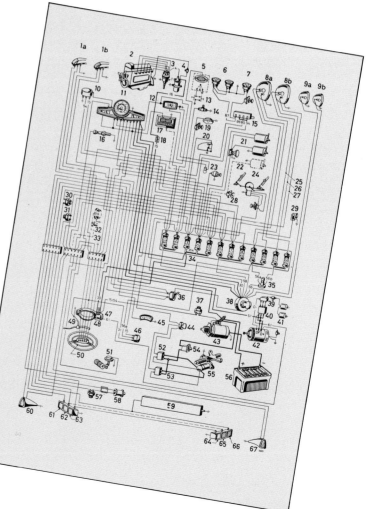

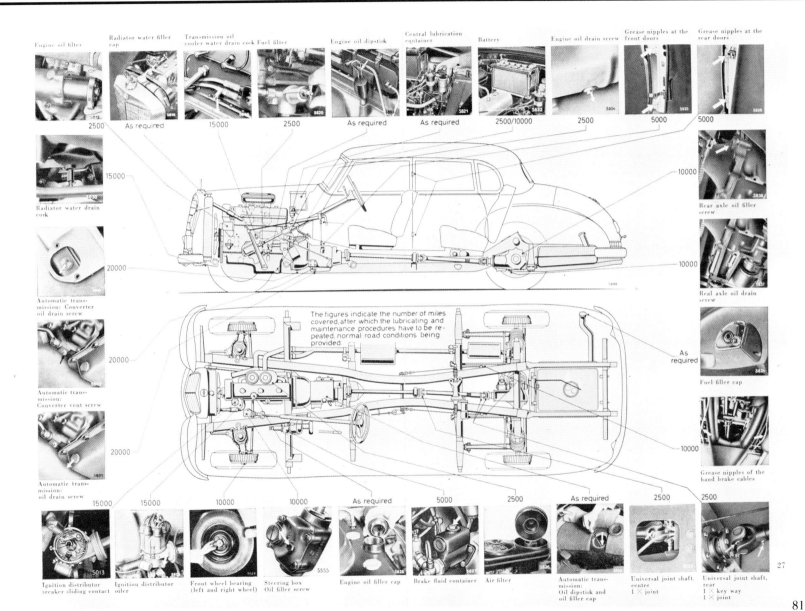

Engine oil filter

Radiator water filler cap

Transmission oil cooler water drain cock Fuel filter

Engine oil dipstick

Central lubrication container

Battery

Engine oil drain screw

Grease nipples at the front doors

Grease nipples at the rear doors

2500

As required

15000

2500

As required

As required

2500/10000

2500

5000

5000

15000

Radiator water drain cock

20000

Automatic transmission: Converter oil drain screw

20000

Automatic transmission: Converter vent screw

20000

Automatic transmission: oil drain screw

10000

10000

Rear axle oil filler screw

10000

Real axle oil drain screw

As required

Fuel filler cap

10000

Grease nipples of the hand brake cables

The figures indicate the number of miles covered, after which the lubricating and maintenance procedures have to be repeated, normal road conditions being provided

15000

15000

10000

10000

As required

5000

2500

As required

2500

2500

Ignition distributor breaker sliding contact

Ignition distributor oiler

Front wheel bearing (left and right wheel)

Steering box Oil filler screw

Engine oil filler cap

Brake fluid container

Air filter

Automatic transmission: Oil dipstick and oil filler cap

Universal joint shaft, centre
1 × joint

Universal joint shaft, rear
1 × key way
1 × joint

27

81

Technical Data

Model	300 (W 186)	300 b (W 186 II/III)	300 c (W 186 IV)	300 d (W 189)
Years built	Nov. 1951 - March 1954	March 1954 - Aug. 1955	Sept. 1955 - July 1957	Aug. 1957 - March 1962
Motor	6 in-line	6 in-line	6 in-line	6 in-line
Bore	85 mm	85 mm	85 mm	85 mm
Stroke	88 mm	88 mm	88 mm	88 mm
Displacement	2996 cc	2996 cc	2996 cc	2996 cc
Compression	6.4 : 1	7.4 : 1	7.4 : 1	8.55 : 1
Horsepower	115 at 4600 rpm	125 at 4500 rpm	125 at 4500 rpm	160 at 5300 rpm
Carburetion	2 Solex 40 PBJC downdraft	2 Solex 32 PAITA Reg. downdraft	2 Solex 32 PAIJAT Reg. downdraft	Bosch fuel injection
Electric	12 volt, 50 Ah	12 volt, 70 Ah	12 volt, 70 Ah	12 volt, 70 Ah
Gearbox	4-speed manual	4-speed manual	4-speed manual	4-speed manual (or automatic)
Wheelbase	3050 mm	3050 mm	3050 mm	3150 mm
Front/rear track	1480/1525 mm	1480/1525 mm	1480/1525 mm	1480/1525 mm
Length	4950 mm	5065 mm	5065 mm	5190 mm
Width	1838 mm	1838 mm	1838 mm	1860 mm
Height	1600 mm	1640 mm	1600 mm	1620 mm
Tires	7.10-15 Extra	7.10-15 Extra	7.60S-15	7.60S-15
Fuel capacity	72 liters	72 liters	72 liters	72 liters
Dry weight	Sedan = 1780 kg Cabrio = 1830 kg	Sedan = 1780 kg Cabrio = 1830 kg	Sedan = 1860 kg Cabrio = 1910 kg	Sedan = 1950 kg Cabrio = 2000 kg
Top speed	160 kph	163 kph	160 kph	170 kph
Number made	Sedan = Cabrio =	Sedan = Cabrio =	Sedan = 1432 Cabrio = 51	Sedan = 3077 Cabrio = 65
Price	Sedan = DM 19,900 Cabrio = DM 23,700	Sedan = DM 22,000 Cabrio = DM 24,700	Sedan = DM 22,000 Cabrio = DM 24,700	Sedan = DM 27,000 Cabrio = DM 30,800

A 300 d with lengthened chassis, rebuilt into an ambulance by Visser of Leeuwarden, Holland in 1961 (H. P. Rinsma Collection).

Model	300 S (W 188)	300 SC (W 188 II)
Years built	July 1952 - Aug. 1955	Sept. 1955 - April 1958
Motor	6 in-line	6 in-line
Bore	85 mm	85 mm
Stroke	88 mm	88 mm
Displacement	2996 cc	2996 cc
Compression	7.8 : 1	8.55 : 1
Horsepower	150 at 5000 rpm	175 at 5400 rpm
Carburetion	3 Solex 40 PBJC downdraft	Bosch fuel injection
Electric	12 volt, 50 Ah	12 volt, 50 Ah
Gearbox	4-speed manual	4-speed manual
Wheelbase	2900 mm	2900 mm
Front/rear track	1480/1525 mm	1480/1525 mm
Length	4700 mm	4700 mm
Width	1860 mm	1860 mm
Height	1510 mm	1510 mm
Tires	6.70-15 Extra	6.50-15 Extra
Fuel capacity	85 liters	85 liters
Dry weight	Sedan = 1760 kg	Sedan = 1780 kg
	Cabrio = 1750 kg	Cabrio = 1770 kg
Top speed	176 kph	180 kph
Number made	Cabrio = 560	Cabrio = 200
	Roadster = 560	Roadster = 200
Price	Cabrio = DM 34,500	Cabrio = DM 36,500
	Roadster = DM 34,500	Roadster = DM 36,500

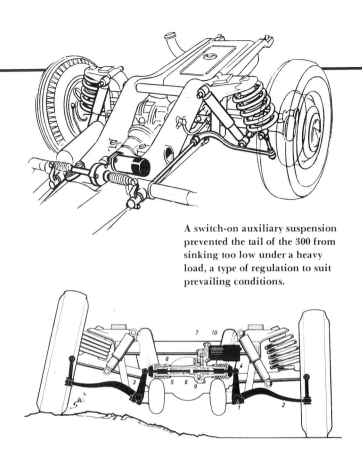

A switch-on auxiliary suspension prevented the tail of the 300 from sinking too low under a heavy load, a type of regulation to suit prevailing conditions.

The 300 as Seen in the Press

In November of 1952, a good year after the renowned Stuttgart auto firm had introduced its big new prestige car in Frankfurt, the journal *Auto, Motor und Sport* became the first to take a closer look at this car that had already gained praise from all sides. Filled with respect, tester Werner Oswald set out to describe the mighty car, and the following sentence fom the introduction to his test report indicates that this test was not exactly meant to discover faults:

"Of course one could think of trifling improvements to details here and there, even on a 300, but placing much emphasis on such wishes in light of the outstanding quality of the three-liter car would be like shooting at elephants with a pop-gun. It would really be unmotivated."

This is followed by an explanatory text on the 300s developmental history and descriptions of technical details, such as the new auxiliary suspension, before the actual testing of the big car begins. The first impression is astounding: "Thus the first, really astonishing surprise is its ease of handling, its maneuverability. Along with these characteristics, it offers extraordinary driving safety and enormous acceleration, so that the sporting driver can slide through thick traffic with the 300, which is otherwise possible only with a spirited but smaller car."

This car's instrument panel holds a mind-boggling number of knobs and levers, but Oswald had no problems in this respect: "It is best for one not to pay attention to these things at first; in time one will get used to them and what they all mean."

After praising the well-functioning heating and cooling system, which at that time could not be taken for granted (most cars did not even have a heater then), the tester took a look at the impressive Becker "Nürburg" radio:

"Developed especially for the MB 300 . . . Aside from its performance, fullness of tone and clear division, this first super auto radio also makes it possible to pick up ultra-short-wave stations. This great super-radio made to pick up the whole world, as its manufacturer calls it, is an eight-tube device with seven wave-length areas and six push-buttons, four of which allow the quick choice of four medium-wave stations . . ." At that time, this was very imposing. In any case, a radio in the car was something very special!

After playing a bit with the alluring controls of the 300, the tester reported on his experiences while driving it, and in every sentence one can hear the pleasure that using this first-class car afforded him: "Really—one must experience it oneself! Naturally our expectations were not modest, but after all, the 300 weighs 1820 kilograms with a full tank. That it walks away from the 220 and even a Porsche under these conditions—that certainly was not to be expected."

The *Ams* team recorded the following acceleration statistics:
0 to 70 kph in 1st and 2nd gears in 9.6 seconds,
0 to 90 kph in 1st to 3rd gears in 15.0 seconds,
0 to 110 kph in 1st to 3rd gears in 20.7 seconds,
0 to 130 kph in 1st to 4th gears in 31.5 seconds,
0 to 150 kph in 1st to 4th gears in 53.0 seconds.

It must be added that at that time there was no faster sports car in Germany. But the 300 was not conducive to rushing. Oswald noted with pleasure: "Over and over we were amused to see how good policemen, when they saw a 300 approaching, quickly smoothed their jackets and seemed to make a hasty move to straighten their belts and ties. After all, one never knows . . ."

Pandit Nehru on a state visit to Germany. Prominent guests were chauffeur-driven in a Mercedes 300 Cabriolet D so they could be seen . . .

Driving this car must have been a very special thrill for its contemporaries, as the great masses of cars, measured by today's standards, were extremely uncomfortable, unspirited and primitive, especially in terms of road-handling and suspension. The 300, though, was very different:

"One completely loses the sensation of speed, as the car moves so quietly, safely and calmly, even on the "main" roads that are often so rough. Where one would otherwise feel quite lightheaded at 70 kph and blame it on the car, the three-liter glides along at 100 as if it were nothing. The reaction of speed-sensitive passengers, particularly women, is interesting. They accept a noticeably greater speed here than in other cars before they begin to object."

But the speeds, astonishing for those times, that this car could attain with ease posed no mean problems for inexperienced drivers, as Oswald acknowledged: "One must pay special attention at night. Far on the horizon one sees one or two points of red light, and before one notices, one has caught up to them. Woe to you if the fellow isn't driving to the right. So one has to be a good driver and have sharp eyes too if one wants to drive really fast."

As for road-handling, it was truly remarkable. Fast action could be taken thanks to the heavy car's safe handling. But at the end just a whisper of criticism became audible: "The car takes curves very properly and scarcely leans at all. Whoever wants to can spin his rear wheels just a bit, as one always has the car firmly under control. One notices only a modest, really very modest lateral sensitivity to trolley lines or superhighway seams."

The Mercedes' steering also earned praise for its directness and precision, which set it apart pleasantly from the wobbly power steering of its American competitors, even though it was linked to a certain heaviness, especially when turning. The form of the

Unser Test:

MERCEDES BENZ 300

Press reports like these were often used by the automobile firms as special editions of advertising literature.

Wenn wir vor ein paar hundert Jahren, schon so weit gewesen wären wie heute, dann hieße das Sprichwort nicht „Kleider machen Leute", sondern „Autos machen Leute". In der Tat: Nie zuvor wurde ich auf Tankstellen so geflissentlich bedient, nie zuvor waren die Hoteldiener so aufmerksam, nie zuvor genoß ich so viel Rücksicht bei VWs und sonstigen respektlosen Wagen wie in den letzten zehn Tagen. Das machten einerseits die in Aussicht stehenden (guten) Trinkgelder, andererseits die Furcht vor den Meterkilogrammen eines 2 to-Wagens und das ergebene Wissen, daß mit „diesem" doch wohl nicht Schritt zu halten sei.

Ja, Autos machen Leute! Und wer mit dem „300" durch die Lande fährt, hat nach der Ansicht der meisten Volksgenossen täglich so viel an Trinkgeld auszugeben, wie es sich ein normaler Mensch im Schweiße seines Angesichts in sechstägiger Arbeit erschuften kann. Wer sich diesen Wagen leistet, meinen sie, muß Generaldirektor (oder mehr) sein, fünffache Abschreibmöglichkeit haben und ist ein so feiner Knopf, daß ihm weder FD-Zug noch PAA vornehm genug sind. Er muß einen Chauffeur und eine dicke Brasilzigarre, in der Diplomatenaktentasche gewichtige Verhandlungspapiere und in der Brieftasche en gros knisternde Hundertmarkscheine haben.

Das ist das Bild, das sich der brave Durchschnittsbürger von dem Manne mit dem 300 macht. Ich wurde des öfteren damit verwechselt, wohl in Ermangelung einer Chauffeursmütze, unter der ich mich als simpler Fahrer hätte tarnen können. Da auch ein guter Ruf verpflichtet, waren es zehn recht „ausgiebige" Tage. Aber auch zehn begeisternde Tage! Wenn der 3 Liter-Mercedes schon ein solches Air um sich gewoben hat, muß ja wohl etwas daran sein: Mit seinen nunmehrigen 125 Pferden der (mindestens bis dato) stärkste und bis dato zum In - Serie - Gehen des BMW 502) der schnellste deutsche Vier- bis Sechssitzer. Wo sich andere Firmen den Kopf zerbrechen, was man im Interesse des Gestehungspreises alles am Auto weglassen soll, hat man sich hier angestrengt, alles einzubauen, was nur irgendwie die Bequemlichkeit der Fahrgäste verbessern kann. Eine Ausstattung, die ihresgleichen sucht, eine unerhörte Fahrsicherheit und Fahrleistungen, die man einem so großen und schweren Wagen kaum zumutet — das sind seine hervorstechenden Eigenschaften, die Grundlagen für vorstehenden ausgezeichneten Ruf.

Da ist zunächst dieser sagenhafte Motor, mit seiner obenliegenden Nockenwelle, seinen schräg in Reihe hängenden, über Schlepphebel betätigten Ventilen, mit 1:7,5 Verdichtung, mit 6000 U/min Höchstdrehzahl und 41,7 PS/Liter fürwahr ein Sportmotor. Gegenüber der Ausführung 1953 hat der 300b noch 10 PS zugelegt und leistet nunmehr bei 4500 U/min gelegt und leistet nunmehr bei 4500 U/min 125 PS. Diese Drehzahl entspricht etwa 120 km/st Fahrgeschwindigkeit, und es ist angesichts der Tatsache, daß nominell 160 km/st Höchstgeschwindigkeit bei rechnerisch 6000 U/min erreicht werden und die Motorleistung dort vielleicht noch 105 PS beträgt, wohl überflüssig zu betonen, welche Leistungsreserven für Beschleunigungen und am Berg zwischen 100 und 140 km/st zur Verfügung stehen. Es ist eben diese Leistungsreserve, die den 300b zu einem Fernreisefahrzeug macht, das aber auch jede Autobahnsteigung im direkten Gang annimmt und oben mit wenig unter 120 km/st ankommt.

Zurückzuführen ist die Leistungserhöhung in erster Linie auf die gegenüber 1953 von 6,4 auf 7,5 erhöhte Verdichtung. Während solche Verdichtungsverhältnisse in Amerika längst zur Tagesordnung zählen, sind sie bei uns doch noch mit dem Odium der Klopfempfindlichkeit behaftet. Mit Recht mißtraut man bei Zylindern von 500 ccm Inhalt solch hoher Verdichtung, wenn mit Normalkraftstoff von vielleicht 80 bis 83 OZ gefahren werden soll. Nun, der 300b

hat einen „Oktanzahl-Kompensator", ein sich geheimnisvoll anhörendes Ding, das aber in Wirklichkeit nichts anderes ist als eine Handverstellung des Zündzeitpunktes. Der kleine Drehschalter am Armaturenbrett wird zweckmäßigerweise zunächst im Uhrzeigersinn bis zum Anschlag gedreht. Je nach getanktem Brennstoff wird entgegen dem Uhrzeiger verdreht, bis sich bei vollem Beschleunigen (möglichst im dritten oder vierten Gang am Berg) das Silberglöcklein unter der Motorhaube hören läßt. Ein leichtes Rückdrehen nach rechts gibt die Gewähr, daß man die Zündung dann nur der weit genug zurückgenommen hat, um klingelfrei zu fahren. Andererseits hat man aber auch die volle Leistung zu haben. Bei Verwendung von Normalbenzin sämtlicher Sorten war der Oktanzahl-Kompensator am rechten Anschlag, ohne daß das Silberglöckchen ganz zum Schweigen gebracht werden konnte, während Super-Kraftstoffe durch die Bank klingelfrei gefahren wurden. Nun denke ich mir, daß sich der Halter eines solchen Wagens wohl auch die fünf oder sechs Pfennige Preisdifferenz zwischen Normal- und Super-Kraftstoff leisten kann, und man eine gewisse Kingelempfindlich-

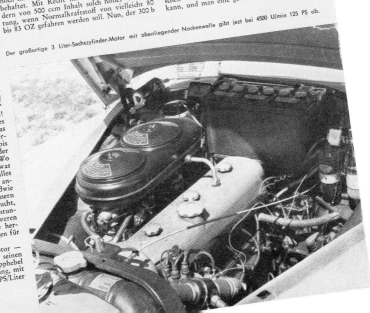

Der großartige 3 Liter-Sechszylinder-Motor mit obenliegender Nockenwelle gibt jezt bei 4500 U/min 125 PS ab.

steering wheel was new: "It is—for the first time in a Mercedes—very attractively made in two-spoke style, retaining the usual horn ring (two- or three-tone horn), but also including the directional-light lever (also a first for Mercedes). An automatic shutoff for the directionals, though, was not included."

As for fuel consumption, the statistics were not bad at all for such a heavy car. At a sustained speed of 150 kph, though, 23 liters of fuel passed through the two Solex carburetors in 100 kilometers. Then the tester ends the article with respectful praise, still obviously moved by the impression that the 300 made on him: "In closing, we can express our joy that Germany, having the Mercedes 300, once again steps to a prominent position on the world market with a first-class product of its automotive industry. Even though this model must be reserved for a limited circle of customers, still its very existence is a significant contribution to the worldwide esteem held by the German automobile. That Mercedes, in building the 300, succeeded at one stroke in creating a truly first-class product is something that they have a right to be proud of in Untertürkheim."

It was also in 1952 that the prestigious quarterly journal *Motor-Revue* had the rare opportunity to test the sporting sister model, the 300 S, a privilege that no other auto magazine in Germany was ever to have; again Werner Oswald was the tester.

Production of this car had begun just a few weeks before, and its high-performance motor produced 150 HP, phenomenal for the early Fifties and only 30 HP less than its direct ancestor, the 540 K, had achieved with a supercharger and eight cylinders. The test car, sportily elegant in light blue with a gray leather interior, did not fail to make an impression: "The external appearance is impressive in itself. The harmonious styling of the wide, low body exudes temperament and good breeding, its classic Mercedes style expresses excellence and prestige. The traditional form may be less appropriate than a modern stressed body, but in a decided luxury car this individualistic attitude is perhaps more important than a potential gain in speed and durability, insofar as the former is quite sufficient in the 300 S anyway, and the latter is of only secondary importance in such cars. On the other hand, they did not insist on a complete change in terms of development, but knew the best way to give a modern aura to the traditional, typical Mercedes style."

The interior lived up to what the luxurious exterior promised. A hardwood dashboard with gleaming chromed dials and switches faced easy chairs that could be adjusted easily to fit any stature and sitting position to provide relaxed riding, pampering the passengers. Operating the Type 300 S coupe, cabriolet or roadster was a pleasure: "The size of the car, the knowledge of its speed, the many instruments, knobs and switches are slightly confusing at first. It is all the more amazing that after driving just a few kilometers one comes to realize that the 300 S is not only remarkable maneuverable but also very easy to control. Aside from controlling it physically and mentally at high speeds, the driver has fewer demands made on him by this car than by many other, more ordinary cars. Along with the outstanding driving safety, the general comfort and the ease of shifting the gears, all of them fully synchronized down to first gear, what stands out is the splendid elasticity and lack of noise from the powerful motor."

Not only in terms of comfort and luxury, though, but also in technical terms, the car set new standards: "The very modern construction of the motor with its overhead camshaft and three downdraft carburetors shows many refinements in design, such as the water and oil temperatures that are controlled thermostatically by a heat exchanger, the automatic auxiliary lubrication of the cylinder walls after a cold start, or the unusual form of the combustion chambers as well as the inlet and exhaust ports. Though such details may not mean much to some people, the effects, namely the performance, elasticity and quiet running of the motor, leave no driver

A faultlessly maintained 300 b, owned by a Hamburg connoisseur. Chauffeur-maintained examples looked as good as new even after decades of service.

unimpressed. When one considers that in direct drive the car can be driven at anything from 25 to 175 kph, it becomes obvious that the essentially high-speed engine will accelerate smoothly and strongly from a laughable 800 rpm."

Driven flat out, the test car reached a top speed of 176.5 kph and accelerated from zero to 90 kph in only 11.4 seconds, figures that lowered all other motor vehicles to the level of mere statistics.

Naturally, such a big, fast car would have been only half as fascinating if the running gear could not handle the enormous engine power. In this respect too, the 300 S was inspiring: "Much more important than the high speed is the driving safety, which remains constant up to the limit . . . The pleasant, not too soft and not too hard suspension guarantees a nearly vibration-free ride under all conditions. Even rows of deep potholes are not felt, even in the steering wheel. The car's easy maneuverability is especially noticeable in, for example, tight curves, because here too one has the car safely under control."

This top-of-the-line model from the house of Daimler-Benz also made a predictably positive impression, scarcely troubled by any criticism, on Werner Oswald, who was usually not impressed so easily, and who summed up the character of the Mercedes-Benz 300 S as follows: The most lasting impression that the 300 S makes on the specialist who is not necessarily interested in buying it is undoubtedly that progress in automotive technology that brought this particular car into being. It achieves performance that formerly was possible only with very heavy cars with large-volume supercharged motors, with much less effort, and above all with a considerably smaller, softer and relatively more economical motor. In the process it offers the best handling characteristics without a hard suspension and is not stingy in terms of roominess and refinements. Just in terms of this consideration, the 300 S is a revelation."

The Type 300 sedan gained ten horsepower in the spring of 1954 through the use of two-stage Solex carburetors, and its brakes were also improved. Just a year later, the Type 300 C appeared, revised again and recognizable by the lengthened rear end. This model could be had now, for the first time, with Borg-Warner automatic transmission. In the spring of 1956, *Auto, Motor und Sport* made a thorough test of this version, beginning with an exhaustive description of the automatic transmission:

"Perhaps it is best to describe the Borg-Warner transmission first. The motor's torque is transmitted from the crankshaft, by either a normal single-plate clutch or the Föttinger torque converter—which can become a hydraulic clutch when released by the controlling mechanism—to the selected planetary drive. This includes two sets of planetary gears, a plate clutch and the band brakes for stopping the individual planetary carriers (for forward and reverse motion or hill-climbing—step one of the selector lever). In all, the planetary gears provide three forward speeds and one reverse, of which the highest gear is, so to speak, the 'direct drive', for here the mechanical clutch is always engaged, while the torque converter or hydraulic clutch and the planetary gears are out of action."

But how did the "Adenauer" Mercedes behave with the American transmission? Presumably no differently from an American car. "Start in position 'O', shift to position '3', release the hand brake and step on the gas . . ." Everything else then took place automatically—according to speed, gas given, resistance. But: "The shifting gaps are clearly noticeable . . . more clearly than we are used to them in American cars." Thus the automatic 300 had only two pedals, and the brakes could—in theory—also be activated with the foot. Which some Americans did, to be sure, but the tester warned against it: "I myself, according to my own experiences, would like to advise you against it, because you can put your left foot, accustomed as it is to the relatively high resistance of the clutch, on the servo-assisted brakes gently enough only after long experience. Braking with the left foot at first provides unexpected braking effects, and perhaps bruises to one's passengers. Whoever in-

A look at the engine compartment of a 300 c. Do-it-yourself work was not authorized, nor was it common—a self-taught mechanic would not have gotten far with the technical complexities . . .

stinctively wants to declutch during a sudden emergency stop and steps on the wide brake pedal will be amazed to find out what power brakes can do."

The functioning of this automatic transmission also caused a few problems in normal driving, and could not replace an experienced and sensitive "stick shifter": "I admit that there are only borderline situations that the automatic can't handle. In any case, though, it follows that strong brakes are necessary with an automatic transmission, quite aside from the high torque of a powerful motor. It is clear that a 250-HP car with 30 or even 40 mkg of torque, even in direct drive, taking an 8-to-10% upgrade at 15 kph, has no hesitation and accelerates smoothly as soon as you step on the gas. But 125 HP and 22.5 mkg are considerably less, and in a tight spot they are just too little." This was attributable to the motor and drive train, the tester added.

Even if this automatic transmission was not perfect, still it generally offered a lot of extra comfort,

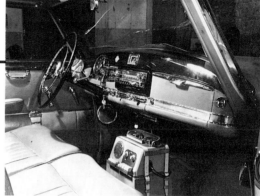

General Lucius Clay on a visit to "his" city of Berlin in 1959.

Above: A look into the cockpit of such a government limousine with UKW telephone.

especially for those who drove often. "It is one thing to drive from Hamburg to the mountains without having to lift a finger to use anything but the horn and the turn signals. And it is no less pleasant to roll along in the thickest traffic at 5 kph without annoyance, to keep up with the fastest and liveliest cars on the superhighway and master any normal situation at all with careless elegance, without taking one's hand off the steering wheel. It is wonderful to stop on a mountainside, steady the car by a light touch of the brake, and then to start up again just by giving gas, without using the hand brake or rolling backward."

Later in the test report it becomes clear that the automatic 300 accelerated almost as well as its predecessor with four-speed manual transmission, and that fuel consumption was only slightly higher than the standard-shift version, all of which was a really positive feature, all the more so with power brakes that could slow the car gently and without a lot of pedal pressure, yet very firmly. At the end of the

test, surprisingly enough, there was clear criticism of several details of the car: "All of this, of course, costs DM 23,500. But the 300 is, after all, the prestige car and not the 220. In view of this prestige, one will naturally miss so many things that have meanwhile become standard equipment, even for low-priced cars, such as directional lights and cigarette lighters that turn off automatically, and flasher lights. One still needs three car keys (starter/ignition lock, left-hand door—the right one cannot be unlocked from outside at all—and glove compartment), the flaps of the pockets in the doors can hardly be opened wide enough to put a road atlas in when the door is closed, and it is almost impossible to get in without dirtying one's trouser legs. Of course standards have risen during the course of the years, but for 23 thousand-mark notes one ought to be able, when buying such a car, to demand a standard of equipment that leaves nothing to be desired."

With the growing prosperity of the German bourgeoisie, the demand for a top-class car had increased, and even Daimler-Benz could not deny it, though otherwise the 300 was treated kindly:

"Let us not forget that the 300 is now five years old, modernized in many ways, but in many other ways still a solidly built car such as scarcely exists otherwise today. Thus it may seem a trifle outmoded in comparison to its younger brothers, but perhaps it simply wants to be something else, something different from them. If the 220, 190 SL, BMW V-8 and Porsche pass it on the Autobahn, still it remains the noble old one that feels greatly superior to the rest of them."

Criticism of the honorable Type 300 did not fall on deaf ears, though, and in the fall of 1957 the 300 d appeared, a flagship that was improved in many ways but, despite the fuel-injection motor and the reinforced body that responded to modern fashion, was still essentially the oldster, a worthy prestige car in the best tradition and of the highest quality. These characteristics, which had become rare even then, led to the Vatican, which had avoided Mercedes cars for more than thirty years, ordering a handmade special version of the 300 for Pope John XXIII in 1960, for delivery in 1961. This unusual car was described thoroughly by the journal *Auto, Motor und Sport:* "It is a 300 with its wheelbase lengthened some 45 centimeters to 3.60 meters, built in the form of a landaulet, a body style not often seen today, with a rigid front and folding rear roof. Front and side windows are considerably higher than usual." In fact, the papal 300 stood 1.72 meters tall overall. But the Holy Father, so it was said, also had a respectable stature in terms of height and width. Using a step that folded out automatically, he could get in standing up, and the rear top, controlled from the driver's seat, could be raised or lowered in no time: "Not an electrically activated top, but the folks in Sindelfingen guaranteed absolute reliability." How electric appliances were—rightfully—mistrusted in those days! "Electrically operated, though, is the individual seat that can be moved forward for getting in and out, with its adjustable back, interior glass and door windows. At his right hand the Pope has the controls of an automatic Becker "Mexico" radio, and opposite him, on two jump seats that appear Spartan compared to his mighty throne but are still quite comfortable, sit his companions. After a formal christening, the car is fulfilling its purpose to the satisfaction of the Holy Father. Two competitors built by Chrysler are currently crossing the Atlantic, to make sure that the Papal blessing is not completely lacking from the American car . . ."

At that time, advertisements like this were still drawn by artists and transposed into mezzotint. This ad appeared in Motor-Revue in 1956.

MERCEDES-BENZ
IN BERLIN

Die Daimler-Benz Aktiengesellschaft
hat ihr seit Jahrzehnten bestehendes
Werk in Berlin-Marienfelde und ihre
bekannten Niederlassungen
in Berlin-Charlottenburg und Spandau
in den letzten Jahren wieder aufgebaut.

Auf dem
**INTERNATIONALEN
BERLINER AUTO-SALON**
vom 6. bis 16. September

zeigte die Daimler-Benz Aktiengesellschaft
die neuen vielbewunderten Sechszylinder-
Personenwagentypen 220 und 300,
die weltbekannten 170 er Modelle V, D und S,
das gesamte
Lastwagen- und Omnibusprogramm
die **Dieselmotoren-Typen**
des Werks Berlin-Marienfelde
für stationäre und bewegliche Kraftanlagen,
sowie für Schiffsantrieb und das
Universal-Motorgerät UNIMOG

Mercedes-Benz in Berlin
The Daimler-Benz Corporation has rebuilt its decades-old factory in Berlin-Marienfelde and its well-known branches in Berlin-Charlottenburg and Spandau in the last few years.
At the INTERNATIONAL BERLIN AUTO-SALON from September 6 to 16, the Daimler-Benz Corporation showed the new, much-admired 6-cylinder passenger car types 220 and 300, the world-renowned 170 models V, D and S, the entire truck and bus production, the Diesel-engine types from the Berlin-Marienfelde factory for stationary and movable power sources as well as for ship powerplants, and the Universal Motor Vehicle UNIMOG.

DAIMLER-BENZ AKTIENGESELLSCHAFT
In writing advertisers please mention the MOTOR-REVUE

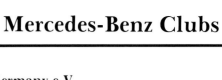

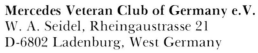

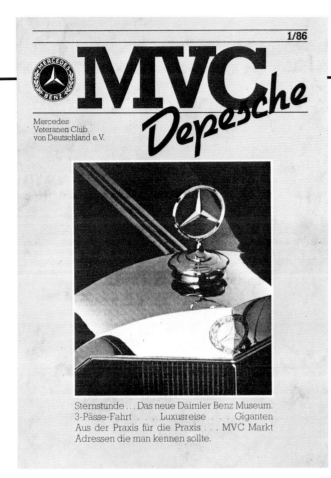

Sternstunde... Das neue Daimler Benz Museum.
3-Pässe-Fahrt... Luxusreise... Giganten
Aus der Praxis für die Praxis... MVC Markt
Adressen die man kennen sollte.

Mercedes Veteran Club of Germany e.V.
W. A. Seidel, Rheingaustrasse 21
D-6802 Ladenburg, West Germany

Bonn Mercedes Veteran Club
Am Kurpark 1
D-5300 Bonn 2, West Germany

1st Mercedes Veteran Club of Oldenburg
Klingenbergstrasse 48F
D-2900 Oldenburg, West Germany

Friends of the Star
Charles M. Ratcliff, Trierer Strasse 58
D-5511 Ayl/Saar, West Germany

Swiss Mercedes-Benz Veteran Club
G. Bürgin, Hegi 242
CH-4625 Oberbuchsiten, Switzerland

The 300 Sc in coupe form is
represented in the Mercedes Veteran
Club by only a few examples. Above
is the title page of the excellently
produced club journal.

Books for the Mercedes Fan

Mercedes for the Road by Henry Rasmussen. A splendid photo volume by this unique photographer in the universally respected Survivors Series. The following models are portrayed: 220 A Cabriolet, 300 SC Roadster, 300 SL Coupe, 300 SL Roadster, 190 SL Roadster, 300 D, 220 SE Cabriolet, 600 Limousine, built between 1969 and 1979. 173 illustrations, 164 of them in color, English text.

The Mighty Mercedes by Michael Frostick. An inclusive illustrated volume from the house of Dalton Watson, covering all racing and production cars from 1885 to 1970. 212 pp, 450 photos, English text.

The Mercedes-Benz Since 1945 Vol. I: The Early Postwar Years—A Collector's Guide by James Taylor. A guidebook for collectors and buyers of early prewar Mercedes. 120 pp, 140 photos, English text.

The Mercedes-Benz Since 1945 Vol. II: The 1960s—A Collector's Guide by James Taylor. A guide for collectors and buyers of Mercedes of the Sixties. 144 pp, 140 illustrations, English text.

The Mercedes-Benz Since 1945 Vol. III: The 1970s—A Collector's Guide by James Taylor. This volume includes the 300, 380, 420 and 500 SL models (1970-1979). 144 pp, 150 illustrations, English text.

Sterne, Stars und Majestäten—Celebrities in Mercedes-Benz by P. Simsa and J. Lewandowski. This book reveals in text and many pictures how generations have been fascinated by the car with the 'star'. 160 pp, 230 b/w photos, German text.

Mercedes-Benz—Klassische Automobile in Wort und Bild by W. A. Seidel. In addition to a history of the firm, the twenty most striking cars of the last 100 years are present in words and pictures. 48 pp, 24 color illustrations, German text.

Mercedes-Benz Automobile: From the 170 to the 300 SL, by Halwart Schrader. One of BLV's six-volume Mercedes set, with exact descriptions of the 170, 220 and 300 series. A wealth of interesting information, technical data and good b/w and color photos. 168 pp, German text.

Zwei Männer—ein Stern: Gottlieb Daimler und Karl Benz in Bildern, Daten und Dokumenten: In the Klassiker der Technik Series, this documentation portrays the birth of the automobile via the histories of its two inventors, from 1886 to the full bloom of the automobile. 485 pp, 46 illustrations, 233 technical drawings, 73 documents and 8 color plates, German text.

Mercedes-Benz by Stuart Bladon. An interesting and pleasant picture volume on the Mercedes-Benz marque. 64 pp, 83 color photos, German text.

Mercedes-Benz Cars by R. M. Clarke, in the Brooklands Series. These volumes are composed of reprints of contemporary articles on the Mercedes-Benz marque. A wealth of historical and technical photo material. Each volume in A4 format, 100 pp, very well illustrated, English text.

Mercedes Pocket History. A small but excellent volume of this popular series. 72 pp, 80 color and b/w photos, French text.

Mercedes-Benz 1886-1986 Catalogue Raisonné. This two-volume encyclopedia was compiled in close cooperation with the Daimler-Benz Archives and other automotive archives. Volume I includes a historical outline, Vol. II lists all passenger cars built by Daimler, Benz and Daimler-Benz AG, with technical data, production figures and body types. 840 pp. in all, more than 100 illustrations, 40 pages in color, 2 volumes in a slipcase, German/English/French text.

Daimler-Benz—Die Technik/Das Unternehmen by M. Barthels, G. Lingnau and M. Kruk. This two-volume history of the firm portrays the development of this significant automobile manufacturer from the beginning to the leading position that the firm holds today. 2 volumes in a slipcase, 628 pp. in all, 803 b/w and color photos, German text.

Mercedes-Benz Personenwagen 1886-1986 by Werner Oswald. This unique book offers an inclusive overview of all the passenger cars built by Daimler and Benz over the past 100 years. Updated edition, 680 pp, 1200 illustrations, German text.

Daimler-Benz—Wo das Auto anfing: 100 Jahre Automobil by Werner Walz. This biography of the firm was issued in its fourth updated edition in 1986. First-class photo material, much historical data from the days of Daimler and Benz. 200 pp, more than 43 color and 201 b/w photos, German text.

Mercedes-Benz—Die ersten hundert Jahre by Richard M. Langworth. A large-format illustrated volume on the complete model development from 1886 to 1986. 256 pp, 341 b/w and 151 color photos, German text.

Mercedes-Benz: A Century of Invention and Innovation. This volume published by the Automobile Quarterly staff shows the high points in the history of the Mercedes-Benz firm. Its contents correspond to No. 24-1 of Automobile Quarterly. 112 pp, 90 illustrations, English text.

The Star and the Laurel: The Centennial History of Daimler, Mercedes and Benz 1886-1986 by Beverley Rae Kimes. This volume, supported by the Mercedes-Benz branch in North America, provides a complete overview of production with more than 750 photos and color illustrations from the Mercedes Archives. A splendid illustrated volume, 400 pp, 782 illustrations, English text.

Mercedes Great Marques Poster Book. A brief history of the firm and the most important models of the marque. The individual pictures can also be framed. 48 pp, 24 color photos, English text.

Mercedes Illustrated Buyers Guide. An informative guide for the buyer, with much technical data and information. 170 pp, ca. 180 illustrations, English text.

Mercedes Color Library/ An illustrated volume in color from the house of Exeter. 48 pp, 130 color photos, English text.

Mercedes-Benz: A History by W. Robert Nitske. The history of the world's oldest automobile manufacturer is portrayed by this American automobile expert. The layout resembles those of the two previous works, "Mercedes 300 SL" and "Mercedes-Benz Production Models." 228 pp, 316 illustrations, English text.

Mercedes-Benz Production Models 1946-1983 by W. Robert Nitske. This new version covers all passenger cars of the postwar era through 1983 and is thus a fully reworked and expanded version of "Mercedes-Benz Production Models to 1975." The appendix includes all the technical charts, production figures and much more. 224 pages, more than 300 illustrations, English text.

Mercedes-Benz Production Models 1946-1986 by W. Robert Nitske. Updated and expanded edition of the book listed above. 263 pp, 349 b/w illustrations, English text.

Daimler-Benz Museum by Fritz B. Busch. This thorough guide to the Daimler-Benz Museum stands out for its excellent color photos and detailed information. 84 pp, 125 illustrations, most in color, German text.

There are a great many models of the Mercedes Type 300, surely very many more than the following list includes. In particular, there are surely a goodly number of promotional models given to chosen Mercedes customers. But since the 300 was not a "People's Car", this car, even as a model, did not achieve the popularity of the smaller production types.

Mercedes 300

Märklin (D)	Readymade	Plastic	1/87
Wiking (D)	Readymade	Plastic	1/87 no windows
Wiking (D)	Readymade	Plastic	1/87 with windows
EKO (E)	Readymade	Plastic	1/86
Siku (D)	Readymade	Plastic	1/60
Märklin (D)	Readymade	Plas/Metal	1/43
Märklin (D)	Readymade	Diecast	1/43
Metal 43 (GB/F)	Kit	Metal	1/43
Solido (F)	Readymade	Diecast	1/41
Prämeta (D)	Readymade	Diecast	1/32 motorized
CKO (D)	Readymade	Tinplate	1/32 flywheel motor
ITC (USA)	Kit	Plastic	1/32
Kleeware (GB)	Kit	Plastic	1/25
Rico (E)	Readymade	Plastic	1/24
Ideal Toys (USA)	Readymade	Plastic	1/20
JNF (D)	Readymade	Tinplate	1/20

Mercedes 300 S/SC Convertible and Coupe

Ariston (I)	Readymade	Plastic	1/43 300 SC Coupe
Metal 43 (GB/F)	Kit	Metal	1/43 300 S Coupe 1955
Metal 43 (GB/F)	Kit	Metal	1/43 300 S Cabrio 1955
Corgi Toys (GB)	Readymade	Diecast	1/36 300 S top up
Corgi Toys (GB)	Readymade	Diecast	1/36 300 S top down

THE SCHIFFER AUTOMOTIVE SERIES

The **Schiffer Automotive Series** features specific models and automobile manufacturers in detailed discussions and pictorial format. Each volume presents a different history of the models chronologically to show their development. Color and black-and-white photographs demonstrate the production, testing, and road use of each automobile. Technical information, contemporary advertisements, cut-away views, and detailed charts of parts and statistics supply important information for owners, restorers, toy collectors, and model buuilders. Each volume contains a list of specialized collector clubs worldwide for the benefit of all.

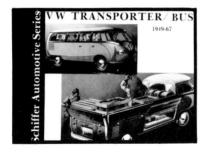

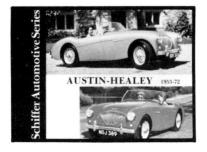

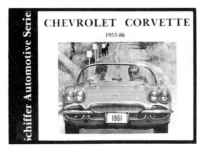